Mississippi Odyssey

Mississippi Odyssey

by

Chris Markham

Northwoods Press

Copyright © 1980 by Chris Markham
No reproduction permitted without consent of publisher
except for brief passages quoted in review.

ISBN 0-89002-165-1, Paperback
ISBN 0-89002-166-X, Cloth

Library of Congress Catalog Card Number: 80-82346

Northwoods Press, Inc.
PO BOX 249
Stafford, VA 22554
USA

IN MEMORY OF
TWO KINDRED SPIRITS
A GREAT RIVERMAN,
WALTER OTIS CARROLL
AND MY MENTOR
MR. STANLEY
OF THE AMPHORA

CONTENTS

Foreword i

CHAPTER ONE
About the River 1

CHAPTER TWO
An Expedition of One 10

CHAPTER THREE
Indians and Dogfish 15

CHAPTER FOUR
On the River 33

CHAPTER FIVE
My First "Snow Job" 53

CHAPTER SIX
On the Run to St. Louis 72

CHAPTER SEVEN
Bridges, Fire and Death 91

CHAPTER EIGHT
To New Orleans and the Sea 108

Acknowledgements 131

Bibliography 132

FOREWORD

Where the overflow from Lake Itasca creates a little brook, forming the headwaters of the great Mississippi River, Chris Markham crossed the Father of Waters in his bare feet, and began his epic hitch-hiking journey downstream to the Gulf of Mexico. Later, backpacking along the roadways of northern Minnesota, he encountered a band of young Indian braves who challenged him by staging a mock war dance around him, complete with authentic war-whoops. Chris sensed danger, but managed to pass it off, and so winning was his personality and obvious courage that these exhuberant young Indians befriended him, and provided him with a ride, right along his course, aboard their jalopy.

Thus begins this incredible story of how the author of this book "thumbed" his way down the entire length of the Mississippi River, proceeding afloat where the great river becomes navigable. The report Chris offers us is indeed tempting, and inspiring. Not all of us, however, enthusiastic as we might become, would have the courage, energy, perseverance, and resourcefulness required to undertake such an unusual venture. Nevertheless, Markham's *Mississippi Odyssey* is a veritable handbook for those who would try it.

In the beginning, there were disappointments and frustrations when Chris attempted to gain rides on the river. By contrast, there were some pleasant surprises, too, perhaps to be earned only by those who possess a persuasiveness such as Markham's. Along the way, he managed to "book passage" free-of-charge aboard a variety of craft, including the modern version of the traditional, floating, drifting "shanty boat," a small towboat engaged in transfer of barges locally, and a big, powerful towboat shoving vast fields of tank and freight barges great distances downstream. It is quite revealing, the way Chris gained official approval from headquarters ashore to ride the towboats, live with their crews, and enjoy bountiful and tasteful meals prepared by a capable, motherly widow, who sat in to play her expert hand at gin with other crew members.

Life aboard these giant towboats is vividly described by Chris, rivaling the candid photographs you will see illustrating his journey. These were taken all along the way, using his loaded and ready journalist's camera, as he passed—and sometimes visited—the towns and cities that over the centuries have become part of the lore and romance of the river.

Arriving at New Orleans, he found his tour almost, but not quite, complete. He then managed to gain free passage downstream for the remaining 100 miles, aboard a big seagoing freighter bound for Casablanca and Algiers. At Pilottown, the Lower River Pilot was exchanged for a Bar Pilot, who always guides the big ships beyond the treacherous bar and out into the Gulf of Mexico.

There at last, where the fresh waters of the Mississippi mingle with the salt waters of the Gulf, Chris disembarked with the Bar Pilot. They returned to a tiny settlement on stilts called "Southwest Pass Bar Pilot Station." They made the run to it aboard the launch in which bar pilots rendezvous with ships off the sea buoy. His remarkable journey was over!

Chris didn't find it easy to make all the arrangements for his unique cruise described in this engaging book. Nearly 2,000 navigable miles of the Mississippi River is a long, long way. Readers who become encouraged to try it may not necessarily achieve the same success as Chris. But they can, at least, find comfortable quarters, southern cooking, and traditional entertainment aboard such nostalgic paddlewheel steamboats as the venerable *Delta Queen* or her modern big sister, the *Mississippi Queen*. Either of these can be boarded at the port of Cincinnati or at numerous cities up and down the Mississippi. But until then, welcome aboard Chris Markham's *Mississippi Odyssey*!

Cdr. E. J. Quinby, USN (Ret.)

CHAPTER ONE

ABOUT THE RIVER

Facts about the Mississippi River usually begin with the emergency of the white man on the scene, as is the case with most histories. Perhaps this is because of some sense of pride of race, feeling that land yet unexplored by white men is virgin soil. But to have a true picture of this river, we must know something of its real beginning and its first peoples. For the settlement of the Mississippi and its valley was an international effort, like the colonization of America itself, not planned and coordinated to reach its all-American climax.

Once, before there was a time, there was no Mississippi River. The angel of ice bared his frigid sword nearly a million years ago and thrust it deep into the topmost half of the North American continent. As the ice advanced and receded four times across the top of the continent, it crushed and tore, gouged and cut the land beneath its massive weight until finally there stood a great inland sea that covered what is now the prairies of Illinois, Missouri and Iowa.

As the crust of the earth shifted, bulging itself skyward here, falling into itself there, this sea lapped at the mountains holding it back from the ocean to the south; other rivers, unnamed, were forcing themselves east and west. Eventually, after many centuries, the sea had disappeared; the Mississippi was born and, with its tributaries, was racing freely to the sea.

Then the wildlife came to the warming valleys and rivers, and with the wildlife came the men—primitive men, who stretched their unknown numbers down along the western edge of the continent; east to the young, great river; and south through the stream's valley to Mexico, Central America, and beyond even to South America.

But these men, called *Bison occidentalis* by modern science, were not the Indians that would greet the first gold-thirsty explorers of the continent. They were late Stone-Age men, hunters of the mastodon and the prehistoric bison, who used advanced weapons for their time—spears, bows and arrows.

For more than ten thousand years these people survived solely as hunters. But then their culture surrendered to new cultures. Minor agriculture and cultivation of wild crops soothed their nomadic instincts, and the arrow maker soon became the tool maker. Thought began to evolve beyond the belly and the phallus; art and imagination entered the lives of these early Mississippi dwellers. And with imagination came belief in ghosts and the spirit world, the awareness of the overpowering mystery of death.

Small civilizations grew and withered along the Mississippi River, leaving behind little to attest to their existence until some three thousand years ago. It was then a new civilization, infatuated with the rituals of death, left its card in the form of great earthen mounds scattered throughout the Ohio and Mississippi valleys. They range anywhere from a few feet in height and diameter to monuments the size of small buildings.

Thousands of these mounds were erected so that almost every modern town along the river has or has had mounds of its own. The mound-builders' civiliation had a long life, as early civilizations go, and vestiges of it remained scattered among a few Southeastern tribes for a time after the arrival of the white man to the continent. But shortly thereafter, for reasons still unexplained, they vanished. They left peacefully, leaving behind a few artifacts and many mysteries; and they left behind the growing cultures of the Sioux, Foxes, Sauks, Dakotas and Chipawas in the North, the Caddees, Wacos, Tunicas, Choctaws, Natchez and Noumas in the South to meet and fall beneath the white man's exploration, exploitation and settlement of the Mississippi.

Although the early settlement and exploration of the Mississippi River is really a French story, it was the Spaniards who first saw it, put rafts on it, and, very probably, were the first to see the river's mouth. But seeking early "Firsts" which have always been the most dominant and marvelous incidents of European history, we must first stand on the marshes of possibilities and assumptions before we can plant our historical feet firmly on the dependability of fact.

At the outset, however, we can be assured of one fact: the Spaniards who came across the Mississippi did so by accident, finding it only as an obstacle in their quest for gold. For only the promise of gold and new riches could lure the Spanish, who had no real desire for exploration per se, into financing their lusty sixteenth-century expeditions.

It was at about the same time that Cortes was setting out to make his cruel mark in history—taking not only the Aztec's gold but destroying their empire as well—that a Spanish navigator by the name of Alvarez de Pineda began his gold-hunt from the east coast of Florida. But a storm forced him westward into the Gulf of Mexico, which he navigated to the eastern coast of Mexico, possibly discovering the mouth of the Mississippi River. Although that is still somewhat speculative, we do know that Pineda placed on a chart of his travels what he believed to be the mouth of a large river. Identifying this river, Pineda named it *Rio del Spiritu Sancte* (River of the Holy Ghost), which, if he did see the Mississippi, would be the first early European name given to the river.

In the spring of 1528, Panfile de Narvaez, governor of Florida, set out to exercise his license to conquer and exploit his dominion. But again a storm waylaid the Spanish from their destination and blew them further into the history of the Mississippi River. Putting ashore somewhere near Tampa Bay, Narvaez and what was left of his original expedition of four hundred men and eighty horses (forty horses were lost in the storm), had the bravado to suppose they could march overland to Florida's southwestern boundary in a few days. In less than three months of battling swamps and jungles, mosquitoes and fever, doggedly attacked by Indians, the gold-dream of the would-be conquistadors died at a point no farther west than the banks of the Aplachicola River in the present Florida panhandle. Their dream now was to live. In a last attempt at survival, the men killed and ate what horses were left; then, with the determination that comes with the approach of imminent death, they sailed five makeshift boats into the gulf, praying to reach Mexico. But the unpredictable gulf quickly swallowed three of the boats, and the other two were wrecked no farther west than the shores of Galveston Bay.

One of the eighty men who crawled onto the Texas shore was Cabeza de Vaca, sent on the expedition to insure the Spanish government's twenty percent of the take. After nearly seven years of roaming blindly through the (present)

American Southwest, it would be de Vaca and three other survivors (Narvaez was not one of them) who would tell of the impelling current of a large river mouth that forced de Vaca's boat more than two miles out into the gulf. We understand his amazement when he still "took fresh water within the sea, because the river came into the sea continually and with great violence."

When de Vaca and his three comrades rediscovered civilization at a Mexican outpost that April day in 1536, they had hundreds of stories to tell, stories of hardship, discovery, adventure and terror; but it was one story in particular that was to send still another expedition to the new world. He had not seen them himiself, but de Vaca had heard more than one tale of the lost Seven Cities, cities with riches never before seen, somewhere west of Tampa Bay.

Hernando De Soto would go to the new world with the largest European expedition the country north of Mexico had yet seen—more than seven hundred men and nearly two hundred and fifty horses. With De Soto and his expedition we are more certain. We know as fact that for nearly two years De Soto murdered his way through the Indians of the Southwest before coming to the east bank of the Mississippi River. Exactly where he first encountered the river is not certain, though it was probably somewhere near what is now Memphis, Tennessee.

Though the determined conquistador could not possibly know it, his expedition was destined to make history with a new set of "Firsts" in the story of the Mississippi. De Soto's sighting of the Mississippi, on May 8, 1541, was the first such recorded observation of the river beyond its mouth, and when he and his greatly depleted army made rafts and sailed them across the river, they were the first white men to perform the feat.

On the western side of the river the army searched for the Seven Cities as far south as Arkansas and as far west as present-day Oklahoma. But there were no lost cities and no gold, and De Soto, with one third of his men and half of his horses dead, decided to get back to the river and sail his expedition to the safety of Cuba.

The defeated De Soto managed to get his men back to the banks of the Mississippi. There he died, probably of malaria. The fact that this great horseman and commander was mortal like any other man could not be known by the Indians, so his men, under cover of darkness, slipped his body into the silent waters of the river. More boats were made then, and a little over three hundred of the original seven hundred sailed down the Mississippi to its mouth and on through the Gulf of Mexico to Cuba. They were the first to do so.

The spaniards had put the Mississippi on the map, but not another one would see the river for more than one hundred and fifty years. And only the Lower Mississippi had been accounted for; the Upper Mississippi was still unknown except to the Indians. It would remain so until the seventeenth century, when the more practical French would discover the "Father of Waters."

The French in the New World differed from the Spanish in two ways: when they began their occupation of New France (Canada) early in the seventeenth century, the wealth of this new land for the French was not gold; it was the valuable beaver pelt. And, unlike the Spanish, they launched no great expeditions against the Indians. Instead they took their wealth by making small settlements among the Indians, conciliating and trading with them. The riches of the New World for the French were tangible, but there was to be one dream. They had not yet penetrated much deeper into the new territory than the St. Lawrence Valley, when they heard Indians tell of a "great water" much further west. This could be nothing less than the Western Sea, across which lay China as far as the French traders were concerned!

Intent on expanding exploration and trade in the new territory, Jean Nicolet, in 1634, headed west, believing that he would reach this Western Sea and China. He was so convinced that he would be greeted by the Chinese at his journey's end that he took with him a silk mandarin robe. The explorer got as far west as Green Lake, Wisconsin. There, dressed in his colorful mandarin robe, he addressed the Winnebago Indians, in lieu of the expected orientals, firing two pistols into the air—thunder to the greatly impressed Indians—at the end of his speech. These Indians told Nicolet of a great water a few days journey away, but instead of pushing on he returned to Quebec with the news that he had gotten close to the great Western Sea.

The belief that the "great water" of the Indians was the mythical Western Sea was to continue for twenty more years. In the 1650's, Medart Chouart, Sieur des Greselliers and his brother-in-law Pierre Radissen set out on an independent expedition through still unmapped country. A few years after returning from their trading with the Indians, Radissen wrote an account of the adventure, stating that "It (the great river)," he wrote, "is so called because it has 2 branches, the one towards the west, the other towards the south, which we believe runs towards Mexico, by tokens they gave us." But this account of the river was somewhat colored with details not based on fact, and it's somewhat uncertain as to whether they were actually on the Mississippi.

Whatever the case, their story convinced the French that the western sea was really a river. But the French still clung to the idea that this river must empty into the Western Sea, or the Gulf of California, which would furnish a route to China. Speculation about the course of the Mississippi finally came to an end in 1673, when Father Jaques Marquette and Louis Joliet entered the Mississippi at the mouth of the Wisconsin and traveled by canoe to near the mouth of the Arkansas. There they learned from the Indians that the river flowed to the Gulf of Mexico. There were Spaniards there, according to the Indians, and they turned back.

Their expedition put the river on the map and ended any doubt of its being and its course forever, though the source of the river would not be discovered for more than another hundred and fifty years.

By further exploring the river, France could have an empire in the very heart of America, could greatly expand her fur trade with the Indians, and from a political viewpoint, could restrict her ancient English enemy to the Atlantic seaboard. Such was the ambition of Sieur de la Salle when, in 1682, he and twenty-three others floated down the Illinois and into the Mississippi, taking their adventurous and ambitious hearts all the way to the Gulf of Mexico. At the mouth of the river, La Salle planted a cross bearing the French coat of arms in the soil of the valley which he called Louisiana, in the name of the French Louis. It was quite an empire La Salle claimed for his France, for in those days a nation which occupied the mouth of a river always claimed all the land from which water ran into that river or any of its branches.

Indeed it was a vast empire the French had claimed for themselves. But the key was to hold this empire, and a string of forest settlements began to line the banks of the Mississippi. In 1717 a tiny settlement on the lower river was established—New Orleans. For not much less than a hundred years the French, whose influence will never be washed away by the river, controlled the entire Mississippi Valley.

But by the mid-eighteenth century France and England, both expanding their territories in the northern part of America toward one another, could no longer remain at peace. War came between the two great powers, and in 1762 France relinquished all of Canada to the British. In a secret move to keep the British from getting all of America, France ceded all of her land west of the Mississippi, including New Orleans, to Spain.

Spain was quick to take control of the Mississippi from its mouth to well above the mouth of the Missouri. She controlled all the navigation of the river, but the people along the river were still loyal to France. Too, the Sons of Liberty were making themselves known along the river, and by the turn of the century Spain was becoming nervous at the great rivers of settlers coming from the east. In 1802 no Americans were allowed to ply the waters of the Mississippi without paying duty to the Spanish, and, two years before, Spain had secretly given Louisiana to Napolean. War was the answer for the new Americans but before it could begin, the Louisiana Purchase settled the question, and the Mississippi River became an American river for all time.

CHAPTER TWO

AN EXPEDITION OF ONE

Unlike other biographers of personal adventures on the Mississippi, I never lived within the sound of towboats bawling for passage around a bend, never witnessed the billowing black smoke of an old stern-wheeler, and never spent boyhood summer days fishing catfish from the river's mud. Instead, I played baseball in vacant lots, roller skated on a dead-end street near a block of factories, and rummaged for near-spent flares along railroad tracks. And though I had thrilled to the adventures of Tom Sawyer and Huck Finn, like millions of other American boys, the magic of the Mississippi was only book-close, as was the excitement of the old West, the adventure of the seven seas, and the fascination of Tom Corbett's galaxies.

But when I was thirteen I crossed the Mighty Mississippi for the first time. I was on my maiden roadway voyage at the time, sent out west to live with relatives, when the driver of the Greyhound bus in which I was riding pointed out the river below as we crossed at St. Louis. I remember him telling me—with great enthusiasm—that "it goes all the way to the ocean, son!" Until then, the only river I had seen was the Passaic, a puny trickle in comparison. I had but a glimpse of the river then; factories lined the banks, and boats and barges plowed through greenish-brown water. I wanted to go down that river, all the way to the ocean and beyond...

Two years later, first hitchhiking east in the back of a pickup, I crossed over the river again. It was then that I promised myself to sail down the Mississippi and out into the ocean someday. At the time I was thinking of doing this on a raft like Tom Sawyer's, and for a moment I thought of doing it then.

But the river would have to wait. I would go east and live with other relatives and attend school for a time. Still a teenager, I would spend hundreds of days and nights hitching the roadways and riding the rails across America. There would be a stretch in the Marine Corps, a reporter's job in North Las Vegas, some success as a photographer; but I would never be able to scratch that itchy foot born so early in my life.

Nearly twenty years later, after more than forty thousand hitchhiking miles, I decided to leave the comfort of my small, attic studio in New Jersey and set out to thumb the Mighty Mississippi; and it was Mark Twain's opening paragraph in *Life on the Mississippi* that made me decide.

"The Mississippi is well worth reading [writing] about. It is not a commonplace river, but on the contrary is in all ways remarkable. Considering the Missouri its main branch, it is the longest river in the world—four thousand miles. It seems to say that it is also the crookedest river in the world, since in one part of its journey it uses up one thousand miles to cover the same ground that the crow would fly over in six hundred and seventy-five. It discharges three times as much water as the St. Lawrence, twenty-five times as much as the Rhine, and three hundred and thirty-eight times as much as the Thames. No other river has so vast a drainage-basin; it draws its water supply from twenty-eight states and territories; from

Delaware on the Atlantic seaboard, and from all the country between that and Idaho on the Pacific slope—a spread of forty-five degrees of longitude. The Mississippi receives and carries to the Gulf water from forty-five subordinate rivers that are navigable by steamboats, and from some hundreds that are navigable by flats and keels. The area of its drainage-basin is as great as the combined areas of England, Wales, Scotland, Ireland, France, Spain, Portugal, Germany, Austria, Italy and Turkey; and almost all this wide region is fertile; the Mississippi valley, proper, is exceptionally so."

How could I *not* go to the river?

But what did I know about the Mississippi? Before I could begin to pack my sea bag and rub saddlesoap into my sheepskin boots, I would have to read about the river, its people.

With histories, travelogs, river lore and geographies I flooded my brain. I collected and studied maps of the river and the ten states it borders or traverses in its 2,348-mile course through the heart of America. Yet, with all this accumulated knowledge, in notes and memory, I was still only book-close to the river. The whole story would not be complete until I had personally plied its waters and stood in its mud.

Too, I knew that in hitchhiking down the river I would be a stranger in not just one but a number of worlds. For the Mississippi River carries the reflections of several worlds, of contrasting life styles and attitudes, as it winds its crooked course from its headwaters in northern Minnesota to its muddy tumbling into the Gulf of Mexico.

One hundred and twenty miles below the Canadian border, in northern Minnesota, lies Lake Itasca, the source of the Mississippi. With several rivulets emptying themselves into it at the south, the small, Y-shaped lake finds its relief at the opposite shore, where the Mississippi is born, flowing quietly and painlessly to life as a small stream no more than a few yards wide and about a foot deep.

With a distinct life and character of its own, the "Infant Mississippi" cuts a crooked course through a forest of pine, fir, and tamarack. A few miles further, running northeast out of the forest, the river winds through miles of thick willows and marsh grass that deny the Mississippi a visible border and belie the existence of the great river. But soon there is a river again.

Spilling itself over minor rapids, winding through swamps and second-growth pine forests, the still-tranquil river easily marries a chain of lakes and pushes eastward to Grand Rapids, Minnesota. There the elevation of the iron-rich Mesabi watershed bends the Mississippi southward and prevents it from spilling away its life into Lake Superior and the Atlantic Ocean.

Steadily the river slices through low walls it has cut for centuries through innocent prairie lands. A host of small tributaries begins to feed into it, and between St. Cloud and the Twin Cities of Minneapolis-St. Paul it becomes—and remains—a mighty river. More than five hundred miles from its peaceful beginnings, the river widens to a quarter mile wide as it flows over the now man-tamed Falls of St. Anthony, at Minneapolis. Here is located the head of navigation and the site of the Upper St. Anthony Lock and Dam, the first in a series of twenty-nine locks and dams that help keep the river open for towboat and heavy barge navigation from Minneapolis to St. Louis, Missouri.

At St. Paul the river is joined from the west by the Minnesota and further south by the St. Croix from the east. The Mississippi becomes marriage of Yugoslav, Italian, Malay,

Chinese, Norwegian, Cajun, and Anglo-American—a blood entwinement that has brought the modern world closer than it has ever been to witnessing the near creation of a new race.

For a man to set out to see all of this is not a new venture; although, it certainly is not a common one. De Sota, Joliet, Marquette, La Salle—men whose names are synonymous with the Mississippi—never realized such a journey. Mike Fink, the hero of keelboat men, and the beloved Mark Twain, who made the river famous in a way no other writer can, never got to see the river from its source to its mouth. Only a few men, in fact, have made this journey. Fewer still have succumbed to the most human temptation, to write a book about it. Though without reading what most have written about the river I could not add my little book to the list.

And so, knowing the might river and its people only from books, I set out to find and feel the pulse of America's main artery for myself, to live a personal adventure on America's river as an expedition of one.

CHAPTER THREE

INDIANS AND DOGFISH

To reach the headwaters of the Mississippi, the obvious place to begin the journey, I walked along the narrow, blacktop road that winds through the towering pines of Itasca State Park.

The midsummer morning was cool, and a soft spectral mist was rolling over the forest floor. Except for the whispers of my breath, the soft cadence of my boots, there was only the sound of the dense forest—bird song, leaves rustling, twigs snapping, a soft wind-hissing in the trees. A fox barked sharply and I looked into the thick underbrush. But there was nothing larger than a few birds flitting about low tree limbs and the tops of bushes.

At the outset, my steps were quick and exuberant. But soon the time between steps became longer, the pace slower. Finally, after I had walked about a mile, I came to a dead stop and unshouldered my equipment: three cameras, two camera bags, a tripod lashed to the top of one of them; an old U.S. Marine Corps sea bag stuffed with clothing, a small tape recorder, medical supplies, mosquito netting left over from a war, maps, notebooks, and a sleeping bag jammed in at the top—nearly a hundred pounds of new weight.

After a short breather, during which time I justified the delay by photographing a wild cluster of blue daisies and the largest toadstool I had ever seen, I pulled the equipment back onto my shoulders and started out again. I paced myself this time and prepared a mental catalog of what equipment I might withdraw from the trip and send home with the first box, brown paper, string and post office I could find. As it turned out, I carried all the equipment through the roughest part of the trip until, in Minneapolis, I shipped home a small portion of my supplies.

The forest to my left began to thin out after a time, and I got my first glimpse of Itasca Lake, nestled placidly in this range of Minnesota hills known to generations of fur traders as the *hauteurs des terres* or "height of land." The day's first light struck the lake, and water stars sprinkled their light through the trees. Two canoers struck out from the shore below me, and they looked as though they were paddling through soft glass.

An hour later, near the most northern tip of the lake, I crossed a small, wooden footbridge and continued on through a narrow forest trail. There, in a clearing, I saw for the first time the uppermost banks of the Mississippi. Approaching the infant river, I thought of the excitement of Henry Rowe Schoolcraft, the man who, in 1832, discovered the river's source.

"What had long been sought, at last appeared suddenly," wrote schoolcraft, the first man to navigate the river from its source to its mouth. "On turning out of a thicket, into a small weedy opening, the cheering sight of a transparent body of water burst upon our view. It was Itasca Lake—the source of the Mississippi."

The Chippewa Indians knew it as Elk Lake or Lac La Biche to the French voyagers who had trapped beaver and mink along its shores for years, though they did not know it

Mother of the Mississippi: Nestled in the hills of northern Minnesota, placid Lake Itasca gives a quiet and painless birth to the Father of Waters.

as the river's source. When Schoolcraft had identified the lake as the source of the Mississippi, he was Indian agent in charge of the tribes of the Lake Superior region. A number of unsuccessful expeditions, in one of which he was a member, had preceded his own. But it was he who sought the birthplace of the river by first asking the Indians. His Chippewa guide Ozawindeb (Yellowhead) was happy to show him the way.

Schoolcraft—anthropologist, mineralogist, author—was somewhat of a classical mind; and when he decided to rename the lake he called it Itasca, a name he created out of the central syllables of two Latin words *veritas* and *caput*—"true head."

A few yards below the river's "true head", I removed my boots and socks and waded into the center of the clear, timid stream, its water sliding cooly around my shins. A small school of Minnows watched cautiously as they hovered against the gentle current near a rock a few yards downstream. There was only a quiet gurgling where this water left the lake, taking on its own character after passing easily through a bridge of stones that rangers have constructed, seeminly an unworthy beginning of the mighty river it is to become.

Feet dried, pictures taken, I rested on a small bench at the edge of the clearing and watched as a family of tourists congregated near the river. One by one they crossed the stones—and the Mississippi—to the west bank, then back again. Two small children left their sneakers on the bank and waded into the brook, laughing and kicking their feet. Their father, lifting the legs of his trousers, soon joined them. He splashed across the stream and back, a round trip of perhaps thirty feet.

By now the sun had climbed above the hills and the forest, and more tourists came into the clearing, equipped with cameras and guide sheets. Soon the few sightseers grew to a small crowd. Some stood near the stream and gazed out over the lake. Others traversed the stone bridge or the flat-cut log that crosses the stream a few yards downriver.

The tranquility of the spot was gone. It was time to follow where the river led. I walked out of the park and pointed my thumb north on US 71.

To travel this upper stretch of river, I had to hitch along the roadways closest to it because, from its source to its official head of navigation in Minneapolis—a course of more than five hundred miles—the Mississippi is not considered navigable. Lost in marshes, swamps, and second-growth pine forest, the river is at best a shallow canoe trail; and where it does become good boatable water, a conoeist must portage no less than a dozen dams. This has been done but not very often. Consequently, I couldn't ride the river here but would have to hitchhike on the nearby state highways and secondary roads until I reached the Twin Cities.

My feet and shoulders were just about ready for me to take a few more pictures when a camper stopped alongside of me. A woman rolled down her window and her husband talked across her.

"Car broke down?" he asked.

"I don't have a car," I told him. "I'm hitching." The man and the woman looked briefly at each other, then stared back at me, not saying anything. "I could use a ride," I added quickly. "I'm headed for Bemidji."

The driver, dressed in jeans and a light jacket, climbed out of the camper and looked over all my equipment. I could see the faces of children peering out from two small windows in the side of the camper. In my earlier days on the road I learned that tourists, especially when traveling with children, are not likely to stop for hitchhikers.

"We're goin' up to Big Fork River," the driver told me, "Bemidji's on the way, so I guess we can give you a lift—if you don't mind riding outside."

With my sea bag hanging over a propane tank secured to the side of the camper, my cameras and equipment bags crossed over my shoulders, I rode for over thirty miles on the camper's running board, clinging to the door and the sideview mirror. By noon, somewhat windblown, I stood near the shores of Lake Bemidji.

Bemidji is a fair-sized tourist town, satisfying the varied tastes of vacationers with fishing, boating, camping and an abundance of souvenir shops. The entire Bemidji area is speckled with hundreds of wilderness lakes. Thousands of campers and sportsmen vacation there the year round. But this small part of North America is best known for being Paul Bunyan country. Until the early 1900's sharp axes and ferocious saws chewed and ate their way through the surrounding pine forests, and the "timber!" cry stretched far across the land. All that remains of that romantic era now, however, is a replica of a logging camp and an eighteen-foot statue of Paul Bunyan and Babe, his great blue ox. Paul and Babe look ludicrous and Disney-like near the shores of the lake. Kiddie rides clatter near their feet.

It is here that the river ends its northward course. Blocked by a low ridge at Lake Bemidji, the Mississippi heads east out of the lake and becomes a distinguishable stream of more than fifty yards wide. Other rivers flow toward the Great

Lakes, but unlike these streams that spill into the lakes and eventually the Atlantic Ocean, the Mississippi turns some fifty miles short of what would be an early death and turns south.

After picking up some canned goods at Bemidji, I headed east on US 2 and managed to hook a ride that took me more than half the seventy miles to Grand Rapids, where I could begin following the more expected southward course of the Mississippi.

The driver, thirtyish, a carpenters apron covering his work clothes, turned out to be from New York. He'd been vacationing in Bemidji four years before and decided to stay.

"I'd been coming out here for the fishing for years," said the driver. "I just fell in love with the country here. It's that simple. I didn't have any obligations, so I decided to stay." He pointed up the road. "There's a rest area over there. You can get a shot of the river."

There was a good view of the river from this small clearing. The river was broader than at its beginning but still stream-like, and I wouldn't have guessed it was the Mississippi. And it was still Nature's river, clear and showing no signs of modern industry.

"Beats Forty-second Street, doesn't it?" he asked. I agreed.

"I have a family now," the driver told me as we rode through the hamlet of Ball Bluff, one of a number of such hamlets that dot the roadways in this mostly wilderness area. "I wouldn't want the kids—I have two boys now—to be raised anywhere else. The people are great, too. Everyone up here seems to know the right thing to do. . .and they do it. They help one another, and I really feel like I live in America here."

We pulled to the side of the road a short distance outside of Deer River, and the ex-New Yorker helped take my equipment out of his trunk. Then from the back seat of his car, cluttered with papers, rope and cardboard boxes, he took a box and tore its side off. He made a necklace of it with string, then with a marker made a sign: GRAND RAPIDS.

"This'll make it a little easier," he said, handing the sign to me. "But you might try standing on the other side of the road. The police pick up hitchhikers pretty quick out here." Hitchhiking in Minnesota on the interstate roads is illegal, and unless you walk along the left (wrong) side of the road the chances are you'll be questioned, if not arrested. Incidents of hitchhikers being arrested in the "Land of 10,000 Lakes" are common, and that misfortune I wanted to avoid. I was thankful for the information.

"Well, good luck," he said climbing back into his car.

"Thanks," I called back. "I just had some."

This part of America is solid Chippewa country, the Chippewas being the only Indians of the Mississippi to remain in any number in the land of their ancestry. At one time the territory belonged to the Sioux nation. For centuries they had the full, uninhibited run of the land. Then the Chippewas were forced from the East by the more powerful and more warlike Iroquois of New York State, whose strength put fear into Indians living as far from them as Iowa.

Naturally, the Sioux were not happy with the encroachment of their hunting grounds by the Chippewas, and for two hundred years Sioux and Chippewas skirmished frequently and fought several major, bloody battles. The Sioux were a large and powerful nation, but they were still living a stone-age culture when the Chippewas, with steel knives and French muskets, routed them out of their lands and forced them westward.

Today the Chippewas do well, having the majority of the rights to harvesting the ever-growing popular wild rice of the region. But the young Chippewas, like all American Indians who have recently been made more aware of the injustices their ancestors suffered at the hands of the white government, harbor a bitterness against the white population.

It was mid-afternoon. I had hitched several rides to a point some thirty miles or so south of Grand Rapids. I was off the interstate and on a secondary hardtop road. The traffic was light but I was happy with it. It was the first stretch of road since leaving Lake Itasca from which I could see the Mississippi from time to time, the road's course running a close parallel with that of the river.

I was trudging along the side of this road, turning back now and then to flag my thumb, when a station wagon suddenly pulled quickly off the road and skidded to a stop twenty yards ahead of me. It was a ride, I was certain, and I half-walked, half-ran towards the waiting car. Before I got there, the driver, an Indian, got out and started walking towards me. I figured at the time he was coming to give me a hand with my equipment. Then a passenger, another Indian, joined him. Three more piled out of the wagon. They were dressed in jeans and overalls, and their black hair was mostly shoulder length.

I set down my equipment and told them I was going as far south as they could take me. They were silent, certainly weren't smiling. I was becoming apprehensive, but I did my best not to show it. I felt like the new kid in the neighborhood about to get a beating from the local gang.

Stopping a few feet away from me, the driver finally said mockingly, "White man want to buy moccasins, beads."

I said nothing.

"No!" another shouted. "How about a nice handmade blanket to keep you warm in winter snow?"

I smiled, thought I should say something, but I couldn't think of one damned word that might get me out of what I now realized was a bad situation. I was thinking of just picking up my equipment and walking right on by them when one of the Indians—all of them looked under twenty-one—screamed a war whoop and started dancing around me. The others joined in, whooping and shouting and performing the mock war dance. A car approached but it shot by without so much as slowing down.

Well, I figured, if they wanted to play, then I would join the game. (When in doubt, punt!) With them dancing and yelling a few obscenities at me, I cupped my hands around my mouth and shouted: "Indians! Make a circle! Hide the women and children!" I then started "shooting" at the Indians with the boyhood gun of my extended index finger and raised thumb. Kneeling behind my sea bag, I fired—"Bang, bang, bang, bang, bang, bang." Six shots should be enough, I figured, and I stood, blowing away the imaginary smoke from the barrel of my "gun."

They were bewildered. They stopped their dance and I very nonchalantly shouldered my equipment and started walking away from them.

"Hey, wait a minute," one of them called to me. "Where you from?"

Turning to face them, I told them my plans, adding that I'd like to make it all the way down the river in one piece.

The driver, who seemed to be something of a leader, nodded and, to my relief, smiled. "Want a ride?" I nodded, though the sooner we parted company the better, I thought.

But my refusal then would probably have invited real trouble. Still I couldn't be certain that there wasn't going to be any after I went with them.

My apprehension was unwarranted, as it turned out, and for an hour we sped alongside the river and bounced over a couple of gravel roads until we pulled out onto Minnesota 210. No one had said very much at first, but after a while they asked me about New Jersey, what it was like, and why I'd left to photograph the Mississippi. The incident of our first meeting was not referred to until they let me off several miles outside of the town of Aitkin.

They helped me get my equipment onto the side of the road and then the driver shook my hand. "We're sorry, all of us." he said, nothing more.

The station wagon swung into a quick U-turn, and I could see three raised fists as the wagon disappeared up the road.

Riding the open back of a nineteen-fortyish truck that was held together with wood strips, bolts and irregular bands of sheetmetal, I reached Brainerd by dusk of my first day hitching the river (I had traveled about two hundred miles). The driver, a weathered-faced old man who said nothing more than "Yup" when he had picked me up, stopped short in the center of town. The old horn honked once. I climbed out and had barely gotten my equipment to the ground when the truck cried into gear and rattled away.

Near that part of town where a small bridge crosses the Mississippi, I walked down to the river bank and found a spot with a tiny stream trailing off the river. The land from the roadside to the river bank was tree-filled, and between two large trees not a yard from the river I found a broad plank someone had wedged between them. Nearby were the ashes of several small fires and on closer examination of the immediate area I found a few remnants of river-side fishermen—a tangled, old fishing line, a rusted fish hook, the rotting scabbard of a fishing knife, some sandwich bags, soda bottles and a few beer cans.

After a supper that reminded me of my freight-hopping days—cold beans and sliced peaches near the side of a stream—I spread my sleeping bag on the plank. With my mosquito hat tied snuggly about my neck, taking my cameras and boots with me, I climbed into "bed" and spent my first night along the banks of the Mississippi—and my last night in the open. I found that the mosquitos aren't really impressed with what you use for protection, and by morning I had gone through nearly half a pint bottle of witch hazel.

At the day's first light, after nursing my mosquito bites and bandaging foot blisters that had swollen beyond band-aid size, I walked to a gas station and shaved. There was a small sporting goods store there and I surrendered to the temptation of buying a light fishing pole, a box of hooks, a bag of weights, a bobber and a small supply of minnows recommended for bait by the proprietor.

After a good breakfast washed down with several cups of hot coffee at a local cafe, I went back to my campsite by the river. When I bought the fishing supplies, I had every intention of fishing in the river's mainstream. But while crossing over the small stream I saw a large fish hovering outside the mouth of an old metal barrel submerged near the bank. Looking closer, I saw that there were a number of such fish spread throughout the length of the stream in groups of twos and threes, some in clear water, others milling around the branches of a partially submerged tree limb. It was a fisherman's dream! Nearly a dozen ten-inch long, mean-looking, hard-fighting fish sitting in a natural barrel, just waiting to be caught!

I quickly rigged my pole, tested the reel, then gave a light cast into the shallow stream. In a moment, I was certain, one of those flat-headed fish—I didn't know what they were—would dart through the water and swallow the hook, line and sinker. Not one of them moved; they were completely oblivious to the wriggling minnow. I quickly reeled in the line and tried again, this time dropping the bait in the middle of the four of them. Nothing! I eased the bait slowly along the stream's muddy bottom until the minnow actually rested a hair's width from the mouth of one of those very "cool" fish. Again nothing. One of them moved finally and poked his ugly head out of the water, gave me a sarcastic glance, jumped defiantly up out of the water and then darted out to the swift current of the river.

After a while, I decided that these fish just weren't hungry or were wise to the hungry look of a man with a fishing pole. Whatever their reasons, I left the fish to themselves. But I was feeling somewhat vengeful. I left that "unlucky pole" resting against a tree near the stream and attached a note to it: "Whoever can catch one of those lazy fish can have this fishing pole and all that goes with it. Please write. Chris Markham, P.O. Box 109, Bloomfield, NJ 07003."

I have yet to hear from anyone who took me up on the offer. Though I'm sure someone has the pole, I wonder if I ever will hear from anyone landing one of those fish.

Still wanting to know what kind of fish they were, I went back to the sporting goods store and told the proprietor what had happened. He was not very impressed but said that from my description they were probably dogfish.

At first I thought he might get somewhat excited to hear of a school of good-sized fish just waiting for the right man to snatch them. But—"if a dogfish ain't hungry, he just ain't hungry," he explained. Mild and unexcited, he went back to straightening his racks of fishing poles.

I told him that I would be leaving then. If he were interested, the "dogfish" were right by the bridge; this news left the proprietor unaffected. Half way out the door I added that I had left the fishing pole there, then headed for the highway and the Twin Cities.

I did a lot of walking that morning, lowering my equipment from time to time, shifting it from shoulder to shoulder. Rides were few and far between, and the few rides I did get never took me more than a few miles at a time.

Before the sun had centered above me, the blisters on my feet burned; a large blister on my left shoulder had burst; and I was hot, tired and speckled with road dirt when I hobbled into a small roadside cafe somewhere between St. Cloud and Anoka. I dragged myself and my equipment to the first booth beyond the door, flopped down and sighed.

There were two young waitresses, a few men eating a late breakfast at the formica counter. No fewer than all of them turned their heads to look at me, each with the same question scrawled across his face: "What the hell happened to you?"

One of the men seated at the counter felt a little embarrassed about staring at me, I suppose, and nodded a greeting. I waved weakly and he came over to the booth. From the tattered condition of me and my equipment he figured I was a hitchhiker, and when I told him I was headed for Minneapolis he said he would give me a ride.

"I've got to make a pickup in St. Cloud first," he said. He was a truck driver. "But if you don't mind waiting a couple hours, I'll take you in." He looked inquiringly to one of the waitresses, a blond with a natural cover-girl complexion.

"He can wait here if he likes," she said. "Looks like he could use the rest anyways."

After she had brought me a second glass of cold beer, the waitress struck up a conversation with me—Where you from? Where you going?—and the talk eventually led to the condition of my aching feet.

"Come on back in the kitchen," she invited, "and I'll let you soak them." My face reddened. "Oh, come on." She took my arm.

As it turned out this lovely angel of mercy had a damn good idea. When I pulled off my boots I found my socks plastered to the skin of my feet in a bond of blood. To say that the water felt good is an understatement.

I was rested, rebandaged and well-fed by late afternoon, but still there was no sign of the truck driver. I was restless and anxious to get to Minneapolis—and my chance to hitch on the river itself—before dark. I waited a little longer. Finally, I thanked the waitress for her kindness—she'd given me a free meal—and started out again.

Walking along the road, stepping as lightly as I could, I was cursing not too far under my breath when the truck driver honked his horn. He'd kept his word, and we headed for the "Water City."

The serenity of the northern lake country of Minnesota disappeared and a broad Mississippi was only occasionally visible as we traveled a swirling tangle of expressways. Then, an hour later, I thanked the truck driver for his extra kindness: He had deviated from his route to Dubuque, Iowa, to drop me off at that point in Minneapolis where the Third Avenue Bridge connects the city just above the Falls of St. Anthony.

Standing on the eastern height of the bridge, I looked down to the rushing waters of a broad Mississippi. I had hitched only three hundred miles to reach this point on the river, but the Mississippi, twisting and looping like a ruptured water spring, had coursed itself through the land for more than five hundred miles before creating the Falls.

To my right was the late afternoon skyline of this city exactly midway between the Equator and the North Pole. A short distance beyond the river's faithful current, huge granaries and mills mark the west bank, the mills' gargantuan bulk outlining a striking mass of stone masonry. In the immediate background stands the city's $4,000,000 Post Office, the Foshay Tower, patterned after the Washington Monument; and in one massive structure of Minnesota granite, the Court House and City Hall.

Looking downriver, I could clearly see the Upper and Lower St. Anthony Falls Locks and Dam, the first of the locks to be negotiated when sailing south on the river. From here on the river is completely navigable for the next two thousand miles till it reaches the Gulf of Mexico. Though I knew the ideal ride would be on a towboat, I was willing to make that journey with the river by outboard, canoe, kyak, or even raft.

These locks hugging the west bank service a substantial flow of both pleasure and commercial traffic, but at that hour there was no traffic whatsoever. Except for its balanced cascade over the man-made dam, the river was quiet and unimposing. The boats I had hoped—expected—to find here were absent.

But I scanned the riverbanks for a spot from where I

At the Upper St. Anthony Lock & Dam, the man-tamed Falls of St. Anthony are no longer an obstacle to navigation. Small harbor tows can travel some four miles above the falls by way of the lock.

might begin thumbing for a ride on a boat, if one should sail by. I saw nothing but private industrial properties. In fact, if there had been any boat traffic, the extensive control of the bank by the private properties would have made it impossible for me to even stand close enough to the water to hail a ride.

As far as the eye could see, the river was off-limits to a lone adventurer. I was sick with disappointment. Still I was determined and resolved as the everflowing river itself to reach the sea. I broke out the maps.

Two public parks, I found, border the west bank of the river not far below the falls—Riverside Park and Minnehaha Park. Standing close to the river's edge in either park, as it appeared then, I would be in a good position to hail any passing boat. I decided to try my luck at Riverside Park. It was close to the Falls of St. Anthony and not more than a mile downstream.

It was still daylight and hot when I arrived at the park, and I sat in the shade of an old cottonwood tree whose roots bulged out of the earth like witches fingers and groped into the flowing river a few feet away. I had barely gotten comfortable when two pleasure craft, outboards running side by side, approached this small turn in the river. I ignored them, however. First, I wanted to get an upstream ride to a point as close to the falls as possible. Then, from the official head of navigation, I would head south.

For a good hour I sat there. I flipped stones into the river and waited in vain for a boat sailing upriver. Finally, I decided that the mile or so to the falls would have to be sacrificed. I would begin hitchhiking southward from here. Many boats had sailed past by then. Certainly I wouldn't have too much trouble getting a ride if I pointed a thumb to the south.

Any number of boats, including several houseboats, sailed

by after that, but I was unable to lure any navigators to stop and give me a lift. Each time I saw a boat approaching, I stood at the water's edge, waved my arms frantically above my head and shouted, "Can you give me a ride?" I never received an answer, yes or no.

Some boaters never even noticed me; the ones who saw me responded only by waving. After a time, it became apparent that my asking for a ride was not audible to boaters so far out on the river. I would have to try at a narrower stretch of this challenging Mississippi. But it was too late to try then. The sun was gone, and the mosquitos were out.

After checking into the YMCA (my self-respect prevented me from presenting my disheveled appearance to a desk clerk in one of Minneapolis' finer hotels), I got myself settled and began sorting out what supplies would have to be forfeited. Getting rides on the river was going to be difficult enough, and I wanted to travel as light as possible. Too, the amount of weight in a small boat would be critical. The combined weight of me and my equipment was that of two hitchhikers, a fact which could prevent me from getting even a short ride in a small outboard or canoe.

Obviously, all of my photographic equipment had to make the journey regardless of its weight. Cameras, equipment bags and tripod would stay. I had an ample supply of note pads, so the tape recorder, which weighed a couple of pounds, would go back to New Jersey. I would keep my blue leisure suit for hell-raising in New Orleans (I was that determined). But the brown suit could be discarded. Tennis shoes were light and could stay. Eliminating the dirty clothing I would be left with three sets of jeans and matching work shirts; I packed the dirty clothes.

And so it went until I had stuffed an empty whisky case

with eight pounds of superfluous equipment and a short note to a friend who would receive this surprise package: "Keep these for me! Will explain later. Having wonderful time; wish you were here with a boat."

CHAPTER FOUR

ON THE RIVER

Seeking a narrower stretch of river the next day, I first went back to my map of Minneapolis and with my index finger traced the Mississippi's paper course until I came to the site of Lock and Dam Number 1, which is actually the third lock below the head of navigation. Tipping the southern border of Minnehaha Park, the lock was three miles downstream from where I had tried to hitch the day before.

The river was still wide here, according to the map's scale, nearly a quarter of a mile from bank to bank, but taking a position just north of the lock might be the best place to try. Any craft heading downstream, be it canoe or towboat, would have to sail close to the bank in its approach to the lock's basin; and upstream traffic would have to run close to the bank for a good fifty yards after leaving the lock. I would wait there.

At a small riverside clearing several yards above the entrance to Lock and Dam Number 1, I found something unexpected—a sign indicating an observation deck for visitors. Perhaps I could ask for a ride from there, I thought, and stepped gingerly down the last thirty yards of blacktop to the observation deck, where a dozen other visitors crowded the rail on the open side—the river side—of the platform. They exchanged a lot of excited comment.

My first sighting of a towboat: The Hortense Ingram *maneuvers her northbound tow into the massive chamber of Lock No. 1.*

Leaning against the rail and looking into the lock basin I saw three small inboards sailing southward out of the enormous lock. But all of the excitement was caused not by the lockage of these small pleasure craft but by something further downstream—a magnificent white towboat pushing northward, two petroleum barges tied head to stern at its bow, its whistle bawling in answer to the all-clear blast from the lock.

As the head of the lead barge slipped between the steel, house-high lower gates and entered the lock, I could see and hear a deckhand calling instructions over a microphone-speaker to the pilot, who remained anonymous behind the polarized sun-shades covering the pilot-house windows. Directly below the visitor's platform, two lockmen hurried along a walkway and quickly tied lines a second deckhand had thrown to them. The atmosphere on the platform fluttered with excitement, and everyone there waved, called out or snapped pictures. The rivermen, however, worked feverishly though systematically, never once looking up to acknowledge their jubilant throng of onlookers.

I wanted to try for a ride on this towboat. If I could get close enough to talk to the pilot, perhaps I could convince him to take me aboard. And if he would soon be sailing downriver perhaps he would take me on again. I shouldered my equipment and looked for a way to get closer to the lock chamber. It was impossible: GOVERNMENT PROPERTY, NO TRESPASSING!

I then hurried beyond the fenced government property and waited in a clearing above the lock's upper gates, from where I would try to get the pilot's attention.

Within ten minutes, 6,000,000 gallons of river had been pumped into the lock basin, raising the water level by thirty-eight feet, and I watched eagerly as the lock's upper gates yawned open. When the towboat had cleared the lock, it moved slowly and hugged the bank. I ran along the shore, and shouting to a deckhand working on the head of the lead barge. "I need a ride."

The deckhand cupped his hands at the sides of his mouth and shouted above the thunder of the towboat's diesel engines. . ."tying up at. . .terminal. . .talk to the captain there."

It sounded like he had said Great Northern or Northwestern Terminal. But I couldn't understand him. I shouted back for the terminal's name, but the deckhand, too, had difficulty understanding. He waved. I waved back and slowed down to watch the towboat plow its tow against the current till its boiling wake disappeared beyond Ford Bridge.

I walked along the bank, checked my maps, but was unable to get an exact location of the terminal where the towboat would be moored. I decided to ask those who must know this stretch of the Mississippi—the Army Corps of Engineers responsible for the locks' operations. Late that day I deliberately invaded the property beyond the NO TRESPASSING signs at the Upper St. Anthony Lock and met Lockmaster Richard Ingle, explained to him my plan.

"Had a couple of boys come through here not too long ago," Richard Ingle told me over a friendly cup of coffee. "They were planning to get to New Orleans on a raft they'd made out of old oil drums and wood planks. They smashed up though, about a hundred miles down, and the Coast Guard had to get them." He laughed lightly. "But I never heard of anyone hitchhiking down, and I've been out here more years than I'd care to remember."

But what about the towboat, I asked. Did he know where she was moored? Could he tell me how to get there?

"The boat you're looking for is the *Hortense*." he said. "Belongs to the Ingram Company, but I don't know how you could get to her through the city." It seemed hopeless. "If you want to try for a ride from here, you can come out on the lock with me and ask some of the people coming down if they'll give you a ride. Be easier than trying from the banks." Amen, brother!

A short time later, a houseboat came into the lock. I asked the owner, a pleasant, thirtyish man dressed in shorts and white deck shoes, if he would give me a ride down to the *Hortense*. He seemed somewhat surprised and apprehensive, but the lockmaster interceded for me and explained why I needed a ride.

"Sounds like a great idea, hitchhiking down the Mississippi," said Cyril Silberman, the boat's owner. "Come aboard."

With a promise from Richard Ingle that I would be allowed to hitch another ride from the lock if I failed to get a ride with the *Hortense*, I climbed down the side of the lock chamber and stepped aboard my first boat on the Mississippi.

Besides Cyril and his wife, two other couples who had joined the Silbermans for a day's outing on the river were aboard the small craft. They were having a small celebration, Cyril told me. He had rebuilt the boat himself, working on her in his spare time for eleven years. Now the *Sangria* was in the condition he wanted. She was neat and clean, its deck soft with bright yellow carpeting, and smelled of fresh paint and varnish. The owner told me that her name had not yet been painted on her bow and that most people at the St. Paul Yacht Club, where he keeps the *Sangria* moored, refer to his little houseboat as the "Yellow Submarine." "But she never submerges," he added for my benefit as we headed downstream.

We slipped under the Old Stone Bridge, a railroad bridge renowned for its all-stone architecture, and soon passed through the Lower St. Anthony Falls Lock. Leaving behind the lock's all-clear whistle and its flashing traffic signals, we floated on a dark and silent Mississippi, the reflection of the *Sangria's* running lights shimmering in the river. The river was beautiful and mysterious, framed by high black banks. I had all I could do to match the reserve and nonchalance of my hosts, laughing and talking, oblivious to the velvet spector beneath us.

About a mile below the falls, the beams from the *Sangria's* searchlights shot through the blackness and danced about the darkened decks of the towboat, which dwarfed the houseboat as we pulled alongside. The *Hortense* looked deserted but a crewman came down from the upper deck, took hold of our lines, and secured them to the towboat.

The pilothouse was dark, filled with the predictable sound of country-western music and what must have been most of the towboat's crew. When I asked for the captain, a crewman used the weak beam of a flashlight to point out a stout man standing near the pilot-house coffee table. I introduced myself. The captain looked nervously about, and I got to the point quickly, explaining that I was willing to work for the privilege of riding on his boat.

"It would be all right with me," said the captain, "but I can't let you on without getting an OK from the company office." He looked to the crewman who was waving the flashlight, examining my equipment. "Think anyone's in the office?"

"Doubt it, Captain."

"Well, give this gentleman the office number," ordered

the captain. He looked back to me. "You'll have to call the office yourself in the morning. I'm sorry."

Pocketing the number, I returned to the *Sangria*. I didn't see the deckhand I'd spoken to earlier, and no one seemed too friendly. I was disappointed and glad Cyril said he'd wait until I was sure of getting a ride. Looking at the dark outline of the forested bluffs lining the river, I could not see a path that might lead back to the city.

A short distance downstream, Cyril steered the *Sangria* close to the bank just above the Lake Street Bridge, where, he told me, I would find a boating club and a road that would lead me back to civilization. As her tiny engines kept the *Sangria* from turning stern-first into the current, I splashed ashore. I thanked Cyril for the ride, then pushed the "Yellow Submarine" away from the bank, its small twin engines churning up river-mud as it forced itself out to deep water.

With everyone aboard waving and wishing me luck, the *Sangria* resumed its southward course and disappeared beyond the Lake Street Bridge, pulling the darkness behind it and over the bank.

Cursing the persistent mosquitos and the dead batteries in my flashlight, I managed to wire a strobe light to one of my cameras. Firing the strobe every few seconds, I groped my way through the underbrush to the foot of the road, a thin V-shaped passageway along the side of a hundred-foot bluff. This road went along the hill northward for twenty yards, then cut thirty yards southwards to the street above. Those last yards to the street above seemed like miles, and each time I set off the strobe I prayed its flash would frighten any snakes that might also be traveling that road. I saw no snakes, however, though dozens of fallen branches had gotten my undivided attention until I left behind the silent river and found myself standing on a Minneapolis thoroughfare bustling with traffic.

My shoulders ached, the mosquito bites were swelling, my boots sloshed with every step, and I would have to spend another night off the river. But I was happy with the progress I had made. I had done it, I had managed to hitch a boat ride on the Mississippi. Though I'd shortened the distance to the gulf by only a few miles, I knew then, that with determination, I would ride the back of this river to the sea.

Determination itself, however, was not going to be comrade enough in making this journey; Lady Luck was going to ride with me, but she would make me sweat to win her smile.

With a large piece of poster cardboard and a marking pen I made a crude sign: NEED RIDE DOWN RIVER. Regardless of the Ingram Company's decision, I would have to hitchhike from the lock that morning. If I got the OK to ride the *Hortense*, I would have to hitch a ride to reach the towboat; and if the answer was no, I would try for a ride with some other boat.

At nine o'clock I dialed the number the captain of the *Hortense* had given me.

At 9:05 I took my sign to the head of navigation, seeking a ride on anything going down river. An Ingram Company representative, regretably, could not allow me aboard the *Hortense*.

On duty at the Upper St. Anthony lock that morning were lockmen Bob Etter and Tim Meers, and Assistant Lockmaster Roger Worth. The lockmaster had told him about my Saturday night visit there and how I'd gotten a ride with the *Sangria*. Roger Worth had suspected I would have to come back to the lock.

"I figured you wouldn't get on the *Hortense*," he said candidly. "It's not too easy to get on a towboat, but I guess you already know that. But if you want to try to get a ride out here, I'll help you all I can. There's one boat upriver right now, the *Mike Harris*."

I was surprised to hear that a towboat was working on the river above the falls. In the early days of steamboating on the Upper Mississippi, daring pilots would navigate hundreds of miles through treacherous channels on the north run from St. Louis to St. Paul, but few of them would brave the dangerous channel between St. Paul and the falls. Passengers bound for St. Anthony and other points north had to leave the boat at St. Paul and travel from there by stage and, years later, by rail.

In the 1850's, however, St. Anthony became the foot of navigation. A few boats were built above the falls, and they brought regular traffic to the upper portion of the river, carrying freight—mostly military supplies, agricultural produce and furs—and passengers between St. Anthony and St. Cloud. Some navigation beyond St. Cloud was realized, but those daring trips were sporadic. Eventually, the shallow-draft steamboats gave way to the heavier and more powerful diesel-powered towboats known on the river today; and, until the construction of the upper lock in 1963, commercial traffic ceased to ply the river north of the falls.

"The tows can go another four and a half miles upriver from here," Bob Etter told me. "But none of the line boats—those are the big jobs that work the entire river—ever come up here though. The smaller towboats, like the *Mike Harris*, shift the empty and loaded barges for the line boats to pick up, usually at South St. Paul. If you can ride with the

Mike Harris," he added, "you should have a good chance of getting one of them down there."

When the pilot of the *Mike Harris* radioed the lock and asked for a traffic report, Roger told him about my wanting a ride. The pilot said he'd let me come aboard—if he could get permission from someone at the company office. He would radio the office and let me know. That was the end of that, I thought. But then a short time later the telephone in the control room rang.

The call was for me. It was Lonnie Jacobs, traffic manager for the Capitol Barge Service, Inc., St. Paul, owners of the *Mike Harris*, and he wanted to have a talk with "that hitchhiker you got out there."

A barrage of questions: Where was I from? Why did I want a ride on the *Mike Harris*? What was I taking pictures of? Was I on an assignment for a newspaper or magazine? I found out later that these questions were more than routine and were asked for reasons other than to determine if I might cause any problem for the company and its insurers, which I had suspected at first.

Two years before, a reporter got a ride on a towboat and wrote an expose for an ecological organization, saying that it was a common practice for deckhands to toss garbage over the side. Since that time, cameras and pens have not received a warm welcome on the river. I was told that the embarrassing incident was the work of one deckhand, and that garbage on the towboats was, as a general rule, burned. On my journey down the river I never had reason to believe otherwise.

"You sure cut out a big job for yourself," Lonnie Jacobs said, after he had again spoken to the assistant lockmaster. "My good friend Roger says you seem to be an all-right guy." (For that endorsement, Roger Worth, I thank you.) "So if you think a short ride on the *Mike Harris* will help you out, then you can go aboard."

I took my equipment to the lock's outer platform, looked upriver and saw the *Mike Harris* turn toward the west bank.

Pushing two open hopper barges of coal, nearly two thousand tons worth, the *Mike Harris* slipped the barges easily into the lock basin. The towboat was neat and trim, with her decks and bulwark painted a bright red, her bulks a clean, fresh white. She appeared docile and humble tied behind the two monstrous barges. But when these "warehouses" of coaldunes were aligned properly in the chamber, the small snubnosed boat became a mini-powerhouse. The three silver stacks behind her pilothouse belched gray smoke-clouds as her engines delivered one thousand horsepower against the river's current, holding the giant barges at bay and preventing them from running with the river and slamming into the lock's lower gates.

Thunder rolled out of the lock as the barges' right flanks tapped the chamber's walls, and two deckhands quickly tossed thick mooring lines to the lockmen. When the barges were securely tied to mooring bits, I climbed aboard the *Mike Harris* for my second lift down the Mississippi, my first on a towboat.

I went to the pilothouse and found pilot Bob Snystad at the controls. He was young, much younger than I had expected, and he was very busy.

"Welcome aboard," he said, raising himself up from the pilot's chair, both hands working the rudder levers, then quickly but confidently adjusting the speed and pull of the engines. "Can't talk to you right now," he apologized while he constantly shifted himself to see out the windows of the pilothouse.

Pilot Bob Synstad works the modern-day steering levers in the tiny pilothouse of the **Mike Harris.**

The combined length of the towboat and the two barges surpassed that of the 400-foot lock chamber, and the *Mike Harris* had to be broken from its tow and tied alongside the barges, with barely inches to spare from its left flank to the opposite lockwall and for the upper gates to close. Then nearly eleven million gallons of Mississippi began to run through the emptying valve, and the deckhands used all their strength to adjust the length and pull of the heavy lines as we descended nearly fifty feet in less than ten minutes.

The huge lower gates eased open, red lights flashed over to green, lock and towboat horns bawled, and we were on our way downstream, quickly covering the short distance to the Lower St. Anthony Lock and Dam. Within half an hour, the Falls of St. Anthony were behind us and we were headed downriver, our barges of coal destined for a "landing fleet"—anchored barges or groups of pilings—at Lambert's Landing, in St. Paul.

"Sorry I couldn't talk to you back there," the pilot said, offering me a cup of coffee. "We're trying to keep up the good time we're making today. On the river, time is money." I was to find this to be true all along the river. Pick up your tow, deliver it, then tie up to another one, and do it all as quickly as possible.

Unlike the early days of barge-shipping, when a line of barges was dragged behind a boat, towboats do not actually tow the barges; they push them. Although relatively few barges could be maneuvered in the old manner, today it is not uncommon to see a line-haul towboat tied to a solid block of barges with a deck area measuring more than five acres, the tow's combined length being greater than that of an ocean-going liner. The smaller harbor towboats like the *Mike Harris* that work the major riverports, however, rarely engage more than six barges at a time, but they work just as hard to move those barges twenty-four hours a day, seven days a week, their small crews of three or four men breaking, assembling and reassembling tows in twelve-hour shifts. On the average, the barges these boats move weigh in at 350 tons and are capable of transporting cargoes—both dry and liquid—in lots of anywhere from 500 to 3,000 tons.

Working the decks of the two such barges being towed by the *Mike Harris* that day were Mike McReynolds, who seems to be making the river his life; Pete Karpin, a college student working for the summer; and Jim Frsby, a young man who likes to travel, sharing a houseboat he keeps moored at the St. Paul Yacht Club with Black, his German Shepherd. Before the river freezes, which it does in early winter, he told me, he plans to sail his houseboat down to New Orleans.

"I don't know if this is the hardest work in the world," Mike told me, "but I've seen a couple of guys come out here and quit after the first day." He laughed. "Sometimes I feel like doing the same thing, but by the time the crew-change comes, I figure it's not so bad."

South of the falls, we cruised easily below two hundred foot bluffs and between cool, forested banks. On the west was Riverside Park, from where I had attempted to hitch two days before. We passed several houseboats heading upstream, their passengers waving and shouting hellos. Tied off at the east bank was the Minnesota Centennial showboat, a stern-wheeled reminder of the golden age of steam on the Mississippi. A short distance downstream, on the opposite bank, children were playing and fishing along the banks; and at one point where the river cuts into the bank to the treeline, a few daring youngsters swung out over the banks from a rope they had tied to a tree. I was really on the Mississippi River.

"I've been on the river about five years now," said the pilot. "But I've never been out here one day when I didn't find some time to admire the river's beauty, especially when the leaves begin to change in the fall. But the river can be dangerous," he added seriously, "and I respect it when it's running hot after the ice breaks up."

He told me that the Mississippi freezes shut, sometimes as far south as the Iowa-Missouri border, from around mid-December to mid-March. Then the ice begins to break on the swelling river, and all along the river the people wait to see the level of that swell.

"There's always some flooding," he said. "But every three or four years the river runs wild and causes all kinds of hell. I've seen it run with as much as twelve or fifteen feet of water through some of the buildings close to the banks." He showed me high-water marks on buildings in St. Paul later that day, but it was still difficult to imagine such swelling from this now docile river.

But what about the locks and dams, I asked. Didn't they help to control the flooding?

"There's not much the locks and dams can do when the river wants to run," he explained. "When it gets bad, there's no traffic on the river, and the engineers open the locks' gates to let the water run; there's nothing else you can do. If they didn't do this, everything above the locks would flood, and the river would just go ahead and run right over the locks anyway."

The main function of the twenty-nine locks and dams that break the Upper Mississippi at intervals of anywhere from ten to fifty miles is to maintain, along with continuous dredging, a channel nine feet deep, a sufficient depth for the towboat and the heavy barge navigation seen on the river today. In the days before the locks and dams, most of which were constructed in the decade 1930-1940, river traffic during the summer or low water months was often brought to a standstill, a fact which helped to minimize the economic growth and settlement of the Upper Mississippi Valley.

Back in the 1830's the Federal Government, realizing the economic potential of the upper river, began the continuous fight to keep the river open for safe navigation. First the most menacing snags, shoals and sand bars were wiped out. Then rapids were dynamited, sloughs and backwaters were closed off, thus confining more flow to the main channel. By the early 1900's Congress declared war on the river and sent the Army Corps of Engineers to gouge snags and boulders out of the river channel, which they were to maintain at a six-foot depth.

The U.S. Army Corps of Engineers now works round the clock to maintain a nine-foot channel in a stream that drops more than four hundred feet in elevation in nearly seven hundred miles from the Falls of St. Anthony to St. Louis. The locks and dams today are like water ladders, storing slackwater pools of river which commercial and pleasure craft can "climb" or "descend" through the lock basins when the river is not frozen or raging high over the land.

And because of this quasi-control of the upper river, the growth of commercial traffic there has been tremendous.

In 1939, when the operation of the Corps' latest project began, less than two and a half million tons of cargo was moved on the Upper Mississippi. Today the petroleum products from the oil fields of Texas and Louisiana, the coal from southern Illinois and western Kentucky, and the grain from the northern states that move on the upper river weigh in at more than fifty-three million tons.

We made our lockage through Lock and Dam Number 1 without delay, though the deckhands were hoping to have to wait for a longer lockage; the better time the boat made, the more tows they would have to assemble or break before they were relieved by the night crew!

A short time later, the pilot rose from his chair, poured on the engine power and quickly worked the flanking rudders. Ahead of us was a bend, which, to me, looked just like any other old bend in this crooked river. Not so.

"This is 'Monkey Rudder Bend'," Bob said, looking straight ahead and keeping a sharp eye on the head of his tow. "It's sharp and always has a strong current."

A late invention in steam navigation on the river, "monkey rudders" were used by sternwheelers in the early days of barge towing. These rudders—sometimes a single rudder—hung just behind the wheel and extended down only to the waterline. Working vigorously in the wheel's tremendous wake, the "monkey rudders" gave a steamer the maneuverability she needed when working sharp bends, especially when towing barges.

"They looked like little monkeys jumping around in the water," Bob explained. "The strong current here took a lot of them to the bottom."

The *Mike Harris* began to shiver violently as the engines strained against the current. "I have to make this bend by what we call flanking." He pointed the barges toward the east bank, and if we had continued forward under engine power we would have run aground. The vibrating stopped and the barges began to swing around the sharp bend. "I have to let the current do the work," Bob explained, constantly working the controls, "If I tried to steer her around under power, the barges would probably break loose." This flanking operation

I would see many times while I was on the river, especially on the Lower Mississippi.

Under diesel power again, the *Mike Harris* pushed her tow down the winding river, and we were soon rounding Pike Island, keeping this island—one of some five hundred such islands in the Mississippi—to our left side. It is here that the Minnesota River cuts through the west bank, with Fort Snelling high on the bluffs above. Established in 1819, Fort Snelling was the beginning of the city of St. Paul. Fourteen years before the fort was constructed, Zebulon Pike bought the property from the Indians for the price of trinkets, sixty gallons of whisky and $200 in cash. Two thousand dollars more would go to the Indians years later as the final payment for the land on which the Twin Cities now stand with nearly two million people.

Beyond, the scenic, forested riverbanks surrender once again to an industrial and metropolitan view. Gangs of barges, moored mostly at the west bank, line the riverside; and on the east bank, well within sight of a river traveler, stands a jagged, steel and concrete mountain range of warehouses, power plants, grain elevators and the modern office buildings and hotels of St. Paul.

Less than a mile below the St. Paul Yacht Club, the deckhands broke the tow of coal barges and assembled a four-barge tow of empties, which the *Mike Harris* then plowed upriver through the three locks and beyond the falls.

We were sailing downstream on this stretch of river when the pilot made radio contact with an upriver-bound towboat. It was the *Itasca*, a trim, blue and white boat slightly larger than the *Mike Harris* with sleeping quarters for its crew.

"What channel do you want, Captain?" asked Bob Snystad.

"I'll take eight, Captain. I'll take eight," came back a metallic Southern voice.

Channel eight is not a river channel but one of the several secondary radio frequencies river pilots use to leave the main channel open for emergencies.

"What kind of a whistle you want, Captain?" asked the *Itasca's* pilot.

"How about one whistle?" On the river, one whistle means that a pilot will keep his vessel to the right; two blasts indicates he will keep to his left. Actually, it was Captain Snystad's choice, for it is more difficult to maneuver a boat running downstream than one moving slowly against the current.

"Sounds good," the southern voice came back. "But I don't know. . . . Let me ask the cook first."

"They have a good crew on the *Itasca*," Bob said to me. "But they're just a little touched." He laughed.

The *Itasca* came back. "The cook is burning supper and don't care what whistle we use. I asked the crew and they don't care neither, and I got a headache and don't want to hear no whistles at all." He laughed, then signaled with a single blast, and the *Mike Harris* returned the signal.

From the *Itasca*: "What are you trying to bring down with that little ol' boat?"

"Got four big ones of coal," Bob told him. "Where you headed?"

"Woo-wee! I thought you'd never ask," replied the *Itasca's* pilot. "Heard you got a professional picture-taker on there. Well, I've been to two county fairs and a chicken fight, but I ain't never got this boat's picture took by a *real* photographer."

The pilot looked to me and I told him I'd be glad to

photograph the *Itasca*. I had planned to anyway.

". . .and the *Santee* is comin' up right behind," the Itasca's pilot was saying when I returned to the pilothouse. "Tell that photographer to watch out for them *Santee* boys—they'll be making obscene poses."

"OK. Thanks," Bob laughed. "Better let you go. I'm coming down on this lock pretty fast."

The pilots signed off and Bob said, "News travels pretty fast on the river. Word about you hitchhiking down the river will reach New Orleans before you leave St. Paul."

Among the rivermen, and the river rats, as the people living along the banks are sometimes called, there are few secrets. Known in the old days as timberhead talk, or sternline talk, news travels north and south on the Mississippi, east and west on its tributaries, faster than the towboats. It gets relayed from channel to shore, from Upper to Lower, from the locks and over the radiophone; and anything out of the ordinary—a hitchhiker on the river, for example—is a welcome curve in the routine line of river work.

By late afternoon we were back at Lambert's Landing, and the deckhands, moving slower now, sweated under the last heat of the day as they secured the four barges of coal to bank-born mooring cables. This was as far south as the *Mike Harris* was to sail that day, never really plying much further south than here; and as I scanned the flat, barge-lined banks I could see there was no sensible spot from where I could hitch another ride. The sun would be down soon and the mosquitos would be swarming hungrily along the banks.

I was taking what I thought would be my last pictures of the *Mike Harris* and her crew when a small outboard with two men moored alongside the towboat. It was Lonnie Jacobs, the man who had given me permission to ride the *Mike Harris*, and Bob Draine, president and owner of Capitol Barge Service.

I climbed down to the lower deck to greet the men, and to thank them for the ride. "Talk to you in a bit," said Bob Draine, who, like Lonnie, is a thick-built man with no time to waste. They walked hurriedly past me and went to the engine room below.

Bob Snystad was giving me an instruction-tour of a barge, naming the different types of mooring devices welded to the barge's deck, when Lonnie and Bob Draine came back on deck and joined us. They were wiping grease from their thick forearms.

"I wonder if Onassis ever got his hands dirty like this," Bob Draine commented, his sun-tanned face twisting to one side as he chewed a plug of tobacco. "I guess my Dad taught me how to work but not to think." I suspect, however, that both he and Lonnie are men endowed with both virtues.

I thanked them and everyone on board for their help. It was near dusk when I asked Lonnie if he could suggest a good place in the St. Paul area from where I could resume hitchhiking.

"Well, that's really why I came out here today," Lonnie said, "even if the boss here did manage to trick me into doing a little work on the generator. It's not going to be too easy getting a ride out here," he warned. "You could end up waiting forever before a boat could stop anywhere out here long enough to pick you up."

I told Lonnie that I had just been thinking the same thing, that I would probably try from Lock and Dam Number 1 the next day.

"I took the liberty of making a few phone calls to some other towing companies," he said. "I don't have any definite word as yet, you understand, but I think I can get you on a line-haul boat, that is if you wouldn't mind staying with us a few more days, two or three at the most."

It was an offer I couldn't refuse.

CHAPTER FIVE

MY FIRST "SNOW JOB"

I remained as the guest of the Capitol Barge Service for three more days, spending most of that time sailing the Mississippi aboard the *Mike Harris*, photographing the twenty-mile stretch of river we plied from above the falls to the Newport "landing fleet" in South St. Paul. I tried my hand at decking, working the forty-pound ratchets and chains the deckhands must use to tighten the wires that hold the barges together. In the near one-hundred-degree heat that rolled up from the deck I learned why some would-be rivermen never stay after the first shift.

It was the morning of what would have been my fourth day with the *Mike Harris* when Lonnie Jacobs came out to the tow and picked me up in a small boat. He took me back to the company office—a houseboat moored at the east bank just north of the Wabasha Street Bridge in St. Paul.

The houseboat-office was a small, two-room affair with several desks and filing cabinets. Though her office bobbed constantly, Dorothy, the company's only secretary, typed and filed, answered the phone or shortwave without the slightest bother.

A few minutes after we arrived at the office, Lonnie got the call he had been waiting for. It was Bob Hertzberg, Marine Superintendent for Cargo Carriers, Inc.,

Minneapolis. Lonnie pleaded my case and gave me that endorsement so necessary on the river today. Then he put me on the phone.

"The *Harriet M* isn't the newest boat on the river," said Bob Hertzberg, after I had answered his own barrage of questions, "and she has a full crew." I had a sleeping bag and was willing to sleep on deck, I told him; and I would bring my own cans of food.

"You won't have to do that," he laughed. "The *Harriet M* isn't that old. And if you're that determined," he said, "I think I can find some room for you. She'll be making the run to St. Louis, but I don't know just yet if I'm going to need her to move further south or not. In any case, the run will take about a week, and I'll try to line up something else for you if I need the *Harriet M* up north again."

That afternoon I left the hospitality of the *Mike Harris* and rode with Lonnie in his pickup to the *Harriet M*, tied alongside several tank (liquid cargo) barges moored at the east bank. Three miles below the St. Paul Yacht Club, the riverfront here is an industrial plain—railroad freight facilities, coal heaps, storage tanks, and a sewerage disposal plant—wedged between the bulwarks of natural sandstone bluffs. On the opposite side of the river sequential runway lights flash from the St. Paul Downtown Airport.

"Good luck and good trip." Lonnie shook my hand and shouted above the deafening chug of pumps and the hiss of giant relief valves on the dockside barges. "Don't let those rivermen snow you too much," he warned with a smile. He had spoken with the *Harriet M's* captain earlier that morning and knew something he wasn't telling. "And whatever you do, don't drink the water," was his farewell advice.

Following a trail of oily bootprints that led through a

tangle of rigging, lines, pipes and steaming valves, I zigzagged my way across the barges moored directly between the dock and the *Harriet M*, a magnificent green and white "queen of the river." I stepped aboard her main deck for my second towboat ride downriver.

Waiting on deck to welcome me aboard were Captain Kenny Hanks, dressed in sport clothes rather than the blue blazer and gold braids someone unfamiliar with the river might expect; Relief Pilot Buddy Howell, cool and comfortable in blue Bermudas, tennis shoes, and a banlon shirt; and Mate Walter Otis Carroll, clad in soiled work clothes, white, short brimmed hat planted loosely on the back of his head.

The captain and the relief pilot, both of them Kentucky men who have worked the river for more than twenty years, had offered a quick and pleasant greeting. The mate, however, with small black eyes and a salt and pepper goatee that gave him a devilish air, offered no smile or greeting when he first took firm hold of my hand. His weathered face was serious, and he used that moment of introduction to study my face closely, intently, as if he were puzzled by something. There was a question he wanted to ask, I could tell, but after loosening his grip on my hand, he said nothing more than "Glad to meet ya." He slowly massaged his little beard and never took his questioning eyes from my face.

"Don't just stand there gaping, Walter!" Buddy Howell ordered with a smile. He seemed to be using great restraint not to burst out laughing. "Help our guest with his gear and get him settled."

Without much effort, the mate flipped my heavy sea bag over his shoulder, looked seriously at Buddy, back to me, shook his head lightly, then led me to quarters on the boat's port side, directly below the pilothouse.

The Mike Harris faces up to transport a few thousand tons of coal to the Newport landing fleet, South St. Paul.

A "Queen of the River:" **The Harriet M.**

The room was small and cozy, with two dressers bolted to the walls, two bunks with a closet between them, a freshly painted radiator, and an air conditioner. The two small windows and the door leading to the outside deck were covered with tin foil, and everything but the green tile floor was painted white. There was a small private shower directly off the room, and on the wall above the paint-stained sink, below the medicine cabinet, was a sign: UNFIT FOR DRINKING.

"If you want drinking water, you can get it from the coolers," Walter said flatly. "We got one in the pilothouse and one in the kitchen. The washing water is filtered river water, and if you drink it, your stomach will rumble all the way to New Orleans." He looked at his watch. "Best forget about stowin' your gear 'til after lunch. Ain't got but half an hour left to eat."

I piled my equipment on the port-side bunk, and when I turned to leave the room, I caught Walter massaging his beard and staring at me with that deep curiosity again. Finally, I asked him what seemed to be troubling him.

"Oh, nothin'," he said, a little embarrassed. "I was just wonderin' if you're really forty-three years old or not." I assured him that I wasn't that old and he grinned. "That's what I thought."

Where did he ever get the idea I was forty-three, I asked. What did my age have to do with anything anyway?

"Well, you'll find out that rivermen like to fool each other a lot," he explained, "and I ain't never met a bigger fooler on this river than Buddy Howell." He looked about the room. "Used to have two real nice calendars on the walls in here—if you know what I mean. But they're all gone now, put away so's you can't see 'em, and all because of Buddy's foolin'. You'll see—" He stopped talking then, and led the way down narrow ladderways and through white corridors to the kitchen.

As soon as we walked into the kitchen, Buddy Howell looked up quickly from his plate, the ends of his thin mustache curling up with a broad grin. First he glanced at Walter and me, then shot his laughing eyes toward the half-dozen men seated at the L-shaped counter. These men, too, clean shaven and neater than I had expected, gazed up at me with disbelief.

"Don't worry, men," Walter said. "Your eyes ain't playin' no tricks on you. Buddy is." He looked down at the pilot, who by this time had burst out laughing. "He ain't no forty-three, Buddy Howell," Walter chided, "and I bet he ain't got no nineteen-year-old daughter just dyin' to meet us rivermen neither."

Buddy was laughing so hard he had to stand away from the counter. "That's right, Walter," he laughed, holding his stomach. "And he ain't got no nineteen-year-old daughter," he admitted as he moved close to the door. "But I got those deck-monkeys to get this boat and themselves so clean they won't be dirty for a whole year."

I was beginning to catch on now, and the men, howling and booing at the pilot, realized that they had been "snowed." They grabbed pieces of bread from the counter and pelted Buddy with them. Walter handed me his hat and told me to "go ahead and throw it" as the "biggest fooler on the river" fled out the back door. With him he took the myth that I was a writer for the *Reader's Digest* traveling down the Mississippi with my beautiful nineteen-year-old daughter! Buddy had provided a light atmosphere for the meeting between myself and the varied personalities serving aboard the *Harriet M* that day, for he knew that intruders were not always welcome.

"I hope you didn't mind Buddy's little joke," Captain Hanks said over a lunch whose menu offered chicken, meatloaf, three salads, fresh-baked bread, and a choice of four homemade pies. "Some of the boys have been on the river over thirty days, and a little bit of fooling helps the morale," he explained. "After a few weeks, a man starts thinking about home almost all of the time. It's what we call Channel Fever."

While the crews working the small harbor tows put in long, back-breaking shifts, they do get to see their families every day; but the men working on the line-haul boats that ply the Mississippi stay with a boat for at least a thirty-day tour and often longer. They work in shifts of six hours on and six hours off, seven days a week and no Sundays, and rarely have an opportunity to go ashore during that time.

"But you'll find out about Channel Fever for yourself," Captain Hanks assured me. "This is all new and exciting for you, I imagine, but after a while you should get a little touch of it yourself."

After Lunch, Captain Hanks gave me a first-class tour of the *Harriet M*, which, like all modern towboats, resembles the old steamers only in size. From her engine room, where powerful diesel engines capable of delivering more than 3,000 horsepower are stationed below her waterline, the *Harriet M* rises through her main deck; her boiler deck, which is a term left over from the old days; her Texas deck, where I was quartered; and her pilothouse, on top of which is a radar platform flanked on each side by a carbon-powered searchlight.

All of the rooms are air conditioned, and the windows and doors in the crew quarters are covered with tin foil, like those in my quarters, to darken those inevitable daylight sleeping hours each shift will have. There is a laundry room with a wringer-style washer and an electric dryer; and there is a recreation lounge with a desk for letter-writing, a card table, a sofa, a lounge chair, and a television that is rarely enjoyed. With only six hours off between often back-breaking work shifts, few rivermen spend any time watching the tube. Those off-hours away from the hot decks and heavy ratchets and unpredictable wires are usually spent cleaning clothes, writing letters or, more often, sleeping. There was one TV show, however, that all of the off-duty crew did keep their eyes open to watch.

"All of us had stayed up one night to watch 'Runaway Barge,' one of those made-for-television movies," Fred Doymer, a young deckhand from Illinois, told me. "It wasn't supposed to be funny, but we all laughed our tails off. The captain in the movie always wore a blue coat and braided hat and was mean all the time. And everyone kept calling him 'sir'."

While I was aboard the *Harriet M*, the atmosphere was always informal. The crew was on a first-name basis with the captain and the pilot—except for the mate Walter. Having worked on the river for more than thirty-five years, and being one of the few rivermen who still holds a Coast Guard license to work as a mate on a steam-powered boat, Walter kept the protocol of yesterday and always addressed Kenny Hanks and Buddy Howell as "Captain"—except when caught in the middle of a snow-job!

In the *Harriet M's* pilothouse, a spacious, cream-colored cabin surrounded by glass, the large spoked wheel of former times has been replaced by levers—levers to control her rudders, levers to awaken or still her engines, and levers to control her searchlamps. A whistle pull hangs directly over the pilot's padded swivel chair, from where, with the flick of a switch, a pilot can extend his navigational senses by radiophone, intercom, radar, swing meter, and fathometer. But left over from the old days is the proverbial coffee pot whose brew is always kept full and fresh by a deckhand.

A few hours before dawn, awakened by the rumbling of the *Harriet M's* engines, I found a serious Buddy Howell hard at work in the pilothouse. Working the engine control levers to command just enough power to hold the boat against the current, he was keeping the towboat's facing knees square against a four-barge tow.

"Check those facing wires, Walter," he commanded over the intercom. Light from the searchlamps poured across the barges. Jeff Mitchell, the relief mate; three deckhands and Walter, who was working into the next shift, strung a cat's cradle of inch-and-a-half steel cable to bind the barges into a single raft. This would be secured to the towboat's flat-nosed bow. "I think I want some stern wires, too, Walter."

Over the intercom came the cry of straining, steel wires; the click of ratchet gears; and the clatter of chains as the crew working the graveyard shift finished assembling the tow. From the darkened pilothouse I caught glimpses of the mate as he went from rigging to rigging, double-checking the crew's work. And always he kept a watchful eye on the young deckhands.

"Lashing a tow or breaking one up is the most dangerous time for the deckhands," Buddy told me as he constantly scanned the barges' decks with the searchlights. "Sometimes a wire will snap, and if it hits a man right, it'll cut him in two where he stands. Or a hawser will pop and throw a man into

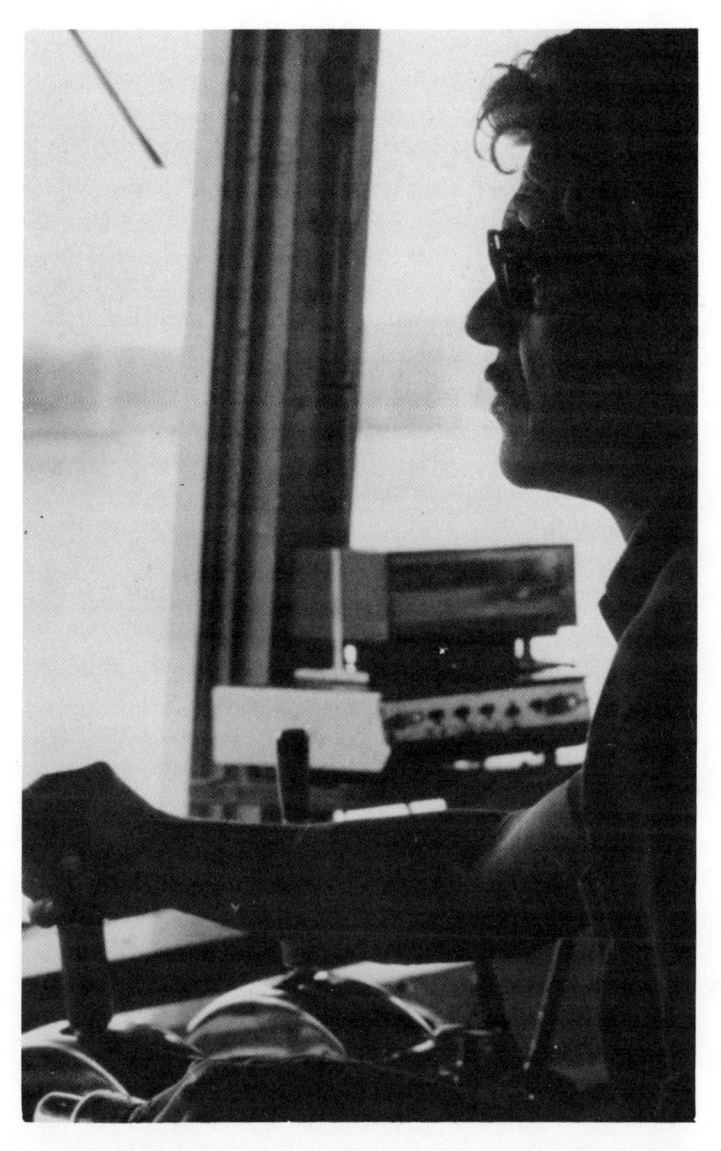

The "biggest fooler on the river," Buddy Howell is a serious pilot at the controls.

the river. They all wear life jackets out there, but a life jacket isn't much good to a man if he gets caught in a strong current or an eddy."

Fortunately, I never saw a man get hurt while I was on the river. But stories of recent accidents and deaths were always with the deckhands. One man that Buddy told me about had recently fallen off a barge during a lockage and was crushed between a barge and the lock's chamber wall. Later I met a deckhand who had escaped with his life when a line had broken. It had only creased him, and he considered himself lucky because he had "only got some scars and lost an eye."

"Working on the river is hard and dangerous work all right," Buddy said. "But I wouldn't want to work anywhere else. A man doesn't belong in an office, accomplishing nothing but waisting his silk for a few people he never meets, and who don't care to meet him."

Buddy told me that he'd graduated college and tried his hand in the cafeteria business with his father before he started to work on the river. That was in 1952. And once, just a few years ago, he tried to leave the river.

"I guess every riverman tries to leave the river sometime," he said. "I left a couple of years back and started selling insurance. I did pretty good, too, but there wasn't a day that I didn't think about the boats; it just gets into a man's blood." He pointed a finger at me. "And I'll bet you couldn't tell me about any other kind of work where a man can start out making thirty-five dollars a day and in three years work himself up to a hundred a day," which is the going rate for pilots these days.

A man who wants to make the river his life and become a towboat pilot someday usually starts by working as a deckhand, learning all he can about the lashing of tows and the behavior of barges—important knowledge for a pilot. After two years, he can take the Coast Guard examination and earn his mate's papers. In another twelve months he can get his pilot's papers by taking another examination, part of which demands that the candidate draw from memory a map of that part of the river where he wants to work. Included in this map must be every buoy, point and sandbar, as well as every bank light by name.

One such man wanting to make the river his life and become a pilot is Jeff Mitchell, a young Arkansas man barely into his twenties. He worked the graveyard shift on the *Harriet M* as relief mate when I met him.

Under Walter's guidance, he'd benefited from more than thirty-five years of experience in understanding the workings of a tow, and had earned his mate's papers. Now, under the wing of Buddy Howell, he gets an occasional chance at the controls.

"It looked easy at first," Jeff told me. "But Buddy got that cockiness out of me. Good thing, too," he admitted. "I'm a lot more serious about it now, and I think I'll be a good pilot in time." I know he will.

Walter gave the signal that the tow was ready and secure. Buddy checked by shortwave for any north or southbound traffic. The river was clear, and the pilot swung the *Harriet M* and her tow 180 degrees into the channel. We were heading south now with three empties and a tank barge load of beet molasses scheduled for delivery to the Anheuser-Busch plant in St. Louis, the world's largest brewery.

"I like delivering beet molasses," Buddy said as we moved slowly down the Mississippi, dark but for the ever-searching carbon lamps, the twinkling of house lights from the banks, and the occasional blinking of the red or green fluorescent tops of channel buoys. "I like to think of it as delivering the molasses to feed the yeast that makes the beer I'm gonna drink when I get my time off."

In the twilight, some three and a half million gallons of Mississippi drained from Lock and Dam Number 2, near Hastings, Minnesota. Soon we were passing the mouth of the St. Croix River, where its clear waters were overpowered by the mightier and tan Mississippi at the small Wisconsin town of Prescott to our east.

Between rolling green hills and high sandstone bluffs we followed the channel that guided us past dozens of forested islands. The rising sun peeked at us from behind the trees.

Captain Hanks relieved Buddy a short time later, and the next shift of deckhands strained at the heavy lines as we made our pass through Lock and Dam Number 3. Several more miles downstream, the marked channel carried us into the broad Mississippi of Lake Pepin. Stretching before us for more than twenty miles and reaching a three-mile width in some places, it is the largest lake between the Twin Cities and the Gulf.

Nourished by the Chippewa River, which flows in from the east, Lake Pepin is a popular playground for fishermen, boaters and water-skiers. The pleasure was high this clear summer day, to the annoyance of Captain Hanks, who gave a four-whistle warning blast to a water-skier making daring zigzag maneuvers fifty yards in front of the lead barges.

"Damn water-skiers," the captain cursed as a teenage boy riding the wake of a small fiberglass boat, thirty yards off our left side, freed one hand from the towrope and waved. "Fool kids got the whole river to water-ski, and they always come into the channel." he said. "And the grownups aren't any better. These people don't realize that if their engine cuts out or if they fall in, a tow couldn't stop until after it plowed right on over 'em.''

Ironically, the sport of water-skiing befits Lake Pepin more than anywhere else in the world. It was here that the now-world-famous sport was invented in 1922 by Ralph W. Samuelson, the first man to strap his feet to eight-foot-long, nine-inch-wide pine boards and glide across the top of the water.

Captain Hanks gave another four-whistle warning, this time to two canoeists who were paddling nonchalantly up the middle of the channel. He sighed.

That night, after I had eaten my first delicious "Gumbo" of shrimp, celery, onions, peppers, and I don't know what else, I met Emma Hogg, the cook and the only woman on board the *Harriet M*. Somewhere in her fifties, Emma was a neat and sprightly woman; and she had just finished giving Buddy, Tankerman Herb Haigler, and Relief Engineer Arkansas Bill (William Garey) their "money's worth" at a round of gin, a daily game the four would play again after the twelve-to-six shift.

"Three years ago, all's I knew about the river was what I'd hear from the men working the canal"—the Intercoastal Canal in Texas—"when they came into my sister's diner," Emma told me as she washed the dishes of fourteen people. "All the men liked my cooking at the diner, and when a cook just up and left a boat one day, the crew came in and asked me if I would cook on the boat for them." She laughed. "They said it would just be 'til they got another cook, but I've been cooking on towboats ever since."

Like most women cooks on the river, Emma is a widow.

She had lived in Australia for most of her married life. But after her husband died, she took her children to live in California, where she put them through college and got them started in their own lives. Then she left the west coast to live and work with her sister in Texas.

"I'll admit I hated it at first," she said. "Cried the first couple of nights I was there. But now I wouldn't want to be any place but on the river. I got one offer though to teach cooks at construction camps in South America. I'm still thinking about it."

"I really like working on the river," she said. "But I wouldn't want to be a pilot. I couldn't drink all of that coffee."

If Mark Twain never said that, he should have.

With its last trails of light slipping down the high banks on the Wisconsin side of the river, a brilliant red sun died in a great light storm behind Minnesota bluffs.

Inside the pilothouse, it was dark but for the eerie glow of the radar screen's searching arm and the giddy light-flips of the fathometer. Ahead of us, a rain of flying insects—"willow bugs," Captain Hanks told me—and a sprinkle of bats danced in the paths of light from the searchlamps that swept across the barges, invaded the mysterious blackness of the banks, or scouted out the marking buoys in the channel ahead. On the barges, the deckhands kept their heads bent against the storm of bugs and moved cautiously about the decks as they checked the ratchets and wires holding together our block of barges.

Captain Hanks and I were enjoying the fresh brew of coffee when Walter came into the pilothouse. "Those willow bugs are dancin' up a storm tonight," he said, spit into a can several times, and poured a cup of coffee for himself. "Can't even talk long enough to tell them deckhands what I want done without getting a mouth full of wings," he complained, "and the decks are gettin' slicker than if they had ice on 'em."

"Looks as bad as that night you pulled old Penitentiary George out of the river, don't it, Walter?" said Captain Hanks.

"Just about," Walter admitted.

The mate, looking like the devil more than ever in the orange light, rested himself on one of the two pilot-house radiators, which was his favorite resting place. He told me that Penitentiary George was not a hardened criminal, as his nickname might imply, but ended up in jail for his drinking and fighting escapades whenever he was ashore.

"Used to come back on the boats to stay sober and out of jail for a while," Walter told me. "He was a good deckhand all right, but he couldn't swim a lick. I saw him fall off the head of a barge on a night just like this one, so I grabbed a pike pole and went slippin' an' slidin' back along the barges—kept pokin' in the river 'til I caught hold of his life jacket and got him back on deck. Like to break my neck runnin' after him."

"Didn't bother old George one bit," added Captain Hanks.

"Hell! I was more shook than he was," Walter admitted. "He thanked me and all, but he told me not to worry if he ever fell in the river again. 'I got it all figured,' he says, 'I'll just hold my breath, get to the bottom as quick as I can, then run up onto the bank'."

Walter laughed. "Old George was serious about that, too. And I'll never be able to count high enough for all the times I pulled him out with that same pole, and him always tellin' me not to worry."

A rumbling suddenly came up from the barges, and soon the *Harriet M* began to tremble. Another moment she was settled again to gliding easily down the channel.

"Must of flattened out a young sandbar that time." Captain Hanks said. He wiped the face of the fathometer, which he calls a pilot's ex-lax machine. "Let that thing read a depth under five feet," he laughed, "and I'll guarantee you a pilot will move his bowels every time. This machine does make piloting a lot easier," he admitted, "but sometimes I wish I had a deckhand out there with a lead line. The old lead line song was a pretty thing to hear, too."

When a pilot wanted a sounding in the days before fathometers, he would give three short blasts of the boat's whistle, and five rivermen would immediately respond. At the head of the lead barge, two men would stand to the port while two others would take up positions on the starboard side. A fifth man stayed in the middle with a megaphone. As the lead line was being cast into the river, the men would call the sounding to the man in the middle, and he would sing the sounding to the pilot, the song of old English being beautifully modulated over the barges and the water.

"Not too many men left on the river who can remember the old lead line song," Captain Hanks said sadly. "Matter of fact, I might get a little stuck myself."

But Walter Otis Carroll, who first came to the river at the age of sixteen, served as a galley boy with a Captain A. B. Fremont, and worked on a steamer with Captain Hanks' father, had the lead line song etched in his memory. That night he wrote down the calls for me:

Quarter Less Twain....................10½ feet

Mark Twain	12 feet
Quarter Twain	13½ feet
Half Twain	15 feet
Quarter Less Tyree	16½ feet
Mark Tyree	18 feet
Quarter Tyree	18 feet
Half Tyree	21 feet
Quarter Less Four	22½ feet
Mark Four	24 feet
No-o-o Bot-tom	

The shift changed as we continued to move steadily downstream. The water-skiers, the pleasure boaters, and the fishermen had left the river for the day; and only an occasional northbound towboat, appearing first as an orange blot on the radar screen, would loom up out of the darkness and blow for a left-side passing.

As the *Harriet M's* propellers churned up the river behind us, we passed small, sleeping river towns. The light from an occasional riverfront house or building would spill out into the river, and the reflection of red and green traffic lights danced their spectrum on the water flowing toward the menacing shadows of the bridges. To the east, on the Wisconsin side of the river, slept the towns of Alma, Cochrane, Fountain City, Bluff Siding and Trempealeau; hidden in the darkness to the west, on the Minnesota side, were Wabasha, Mineiska, Minnesota City, and the city of Winona.

One hundred miles below St. Paul, Winona is planted firmly in hardwood country. Feeding itself from the surrounding forests, the city grew and later offered education with the first normal school west of the Mississippi. On the site today stands Winona State College. The forests eventually surrendered the last of their economic yield, and today the city survives with the manufacturing of varied products ranging from candy to sauerkraut, wooden boxes to fur garments, auto chains to rock drills. But to the early river pilots the city was known for Sugar Loaf, one of its massive limestone bluffs towering hundreds of feet above the river. It was once a landmark by which pilots used to steer, but now the top of 600-foot bluff—and the tops of the other bluffs—is used as a lookout post by the men of the Upper Mississippi River Wildlife and Fish Refuge. They watch for miles around for picknickers who might miss the trash cans!

In the first light of the next day, we passed the city of LaCrosse, Wisconsin, which three-quarters of a century ago depleted the surrounding forests and left to history its early logging and sawmill industries. On the Mississippi at the confluence of the Black River and LaCrosse Creek, the city now relies on the tourist trade as well as the manufacture of air-conditioners and farm equipment, automobile parts and plastics.

A few miles downstream from LaCrosse, we encountered a misty Mississippi near Stoddard, Wisconsin. Here the outboard john boats of commercial fishermen stirred up the water in the narrow channels that map themselves between fields of giant lily pads. The men—usually one or two to a boat—work their skiffs from net to net, and bring in a catch of large carp or buffalo.

Two fishermen from Stoddard working their nets that day were fifteen-year-old Barry Haydysch and his brother Brian. They were "gill fishing", using twenty-yard-long, rectangular nets with square, seven-inch openings. They had stretched these nets across the channels between the lily pads the night before. Any carp, buffalo, or catfish not large enough to pass

Carp in a gill net: A few of the 50 million pounds of fresh water fish that finds its way from the Mississippi to the American market each year.

through the nets, which are tied to long tree limbs the fishermen push deep into the muddy bottom, are pulled onto a large flat board at the bow of the boat, clubbed with a large stick, and tossed into the boat's well, where they lay stunned before delivery to the wholesaler.

In their tiny skiffs, full-time commercial fishermen on the Mississippi, and the part-timers like Brian and Barry, who helps his brother with the morning catch before he leaves for school, last year delivered more than fifty million pounds of fresh-water fish to the commercial market.

Commercial clammers, using much larger boats, work the river's clam beds and each year pull in tons of clams whose shells find ready buyers on the Japanese market. After dicing and tumbling the shells into tiny spheres, the Japanese pearl manufacturers implant these little "nuggets" into oysters which wait, perhaps not so eagerly, to coat the irritants from the Mississippi with thin layers of nacre to form pearls.

Under the watchful eyes of the fishermen, who are less than fond of the towboats "spoiling the river," we continued southward and left in our wake the state of Minnesota. Iowa was on our right now, and Wisconsin bordered us on our left for nearly another mile before we passed the banks of the Wisconsin-Illinois border. Here, on the Illinois side of the river, lies the small town of East Dubuque. On the west bank is the oldest city in Iowa, Dubuque, whose busy riverport is winter quarters for many of the boats that work the Upper Mississippi in the spring and summer.

We had sailed steadily and without delay since we first left St. Paul, but a few miles downstream from Dubuque we met a thick, rolling fog and had to run for the safety of an Iowa bank. There we tied off for the night and well into the morning of the next day.

"No matter how much radar and 'razmatazz' equipment you put on the boats," Buddy declared, "if the river wants to clear its channels for the night it can."

We were in the pilothouse, watching Walter and the deckhands as they worked free the heavy lines they had knotted around the trunks of thick trees the night before.

"A good heavy fog stops everything on the river, just like it did in the old days before all the fancy equipment," Buddy was saying when suddenly we heard the wild shouting of the men on deck and on the bank.

Looking out through the front glass of the pilothouse, we saw Walter throw the last line sloppily onto the deck of the lead barge and mount in two amazing leaps. Then, hat in hand, he ran close behind the gang of fleeing deckhands, all of whom thrashed their arms wildly over their heads and shoulders as they dashed for cover.

Walter triple-jumped the boat's forward ladders, darted into the pilothouse, and slammed the door shut behind him. Outside, the pilothouse windows beat with the tattoo of an army of angry insects each the size of a man's thumb. They were looking for Walter and his crew.

"Damn!" Walter said as he rubbed his chest. "Damn! Those Japanese hornets sure carry a wallop." He had been stung in the chest three times before making it to the safety of the pilothouse. "I was so busy lookin' out for snakes I never gave a thought to that hornets nest 'til it was too late."

Buddy moved the *Harriet M* slowly out from the bank and into the channel. Eventually, the hornets lost interest. Walter, however, would not feel like himself for several more days. Now his experience is a new story they tell some nights in the pilothouse—how old Walter had "jumped from the bank like a woman with a snapped girdle."

CHAPTER SIX

ON THE RUN TO ST. LOUIS

A thin but steady line of northbound tows whistled for passing as we rolled between riverbanks whose limestone bluffs stood wider apart now, with natural forests and rich farmlands wedged between them. Farmhouses blinked at us from behind the thin, riverside forests from time to time; but there was a tight string of riverfront homes, most of which stood bravely on wooden stilts or tops of concrete walls, as we glided easily beyond the iron works and machine shops of Clinton, Iowa. By nightfall, we were moving slowly into the busy channel where the banks are cluttered with the industry of the Quad Cities: Rock Island, Moline and East Moline, Illinois and Davenport, Iowa.

Locking through basins wider than those of the Panama Canal, we sailed safely beneath the Rock Island bridge. Though no longer a threat to them, it is hated by every riverman. It was at this bridge that, in the spring of 1856, the long-lasting feud between the railroads and the towboat companies began.

Less than three weeks after the first locomotive puffed across the Rock Island bridge, the first railroad bridge to span the Mississippi, the steamboat *Effie Afton* headed north from her port at Davenport, Iowa, and quickly entered the channel flowing beneath the bridge. It was "pilot error," according to the Rock Island Railroad, that sent the ill-fated steamboat slamming into one of the bridge piers, bursting her into flames, burning her decks down to the waterline. But the boat's owners claimed that the bridge was an unlawful and unnatural obstruction to navigation, and they sued the railroad.

With the aid of three lawyers for the defense, the Rock Island Railroad won the case. One of those lawyers was an attorney from Springfield, Illinois. His name was Abraham Lincoln.

After Lincoln had personally inspected the bridge, took his own measurements, the lawyer who would become President in five more years added to the defense a statement that would later be known in the Supreme Court as a Lincoln Doctrine: ". . .A man has a good right to go across a river as another has to go up or down the river. . . the existence of a bridge which does not prevent or unreasonably obstruct navigation is not inconsistent with the navigable character of the stream."

Today, sailing through the safety of locks, thousands of modern towboats push thousands of barges that carry millions of tons of cargo each year under the Rock Island bridge without incident. But though the Rock Island Line might be a mighty fine line, you'll never hear it from a riverman.

Less than ten miles below the mouth of the Rock River, Buddy turned the *Harriet M* out of the channel and guided her to a landing fleet at the west bank near Buffalo, Iowa, a small town which was once a favored residence for steamboat pilots. The town was asleep, and the bank was dark and quiet.

But our block of barges and the landing fleet were busy islands of steel as Jeff Mitchell and his crew, spotlighted by searchlamp beams cutting through a living screen of willow bugs and mosquitos, strung new lines and wires, cranked stiff ratchet arms, and turned large winch wheels to secure three more barges to our tow.

After more than two hours of steady work for both crew and pilot—the deckhands' safety depended on Buddy's constant attention and skill during the lashing operation—Buddy steered the *Harriet M* into the channel, and soon we were moving seven barges on the run to St. Louis.

The new barges were empties, but their combined weight added more than another thousand tons to our tow. For Captain Hanks and Buddy this new tonnage would mean more difficult handling in the bends and crossings of the river to come, and for the deckhands our tow's new length—nearly three hundred yards—would mean more time for them to sweat on the hot decks by day, more dangerous watches on the barges by night.

Before we would reach the busy riverport of St. Louis, which is just below the last lock we would negotiate on our southward course, we would have to sail through eleven more locks. Of these, only two locks—Number 19, at Keokuk, Iowa, and the final lock, Number 27, at Granite City, Illinois—would have a chamber-length capable of taking us through with a single locking operation. All the others would have to be made with double lockings, when the deckhands would have to split the tow before each lockage, then reassemble it afterwards.

A double locking operation is a long (about an hour and a half) and tedious chore, and at the shift-change the next morning some of the deckhands grumbled a little as they flocked around the pilot's maps and tried to estimate how many of the nine double lockings each shift might catch.

"You'll find out what locks you gotta make when you get to 'em," Walter teased. "You'll have the boys back east thinkin' rivermen don't like workin', so stop pussyfootin' round them maps, and get busy soochin' them decks and these windows."

The men, still calculating mileages and possible lock delays, scrambled out of the pilothouse. Walter sat in the small, leather lounge at the rear of the pilothouse and spread a day-old Sunday newspaper across his lap.

"I wonder what they woulda done if they hadda go out on them barges with pound-and-a-half hail stones fallin' on 'em," he said, shaking his head, "like I done one day back in the fifties. Those hail stones were as big as cannon balls—hit the trees on one of them islands and cleared a path so big you could take a boat through if it had water on it," Walter told me. Captain Hanks, pouring a cup of coffee, gave the mate a sideways glance, then screwed up his eyes. He'd heard this one before!

"I had to go out there and tie up the barges with one hand," Walter continued, "and hold a GI can lid over my head with the other to keep them ice balls from knockin' my head clean off." He then adjusted his small, wire-rimmed reading glasses and began leafing through the newspaper. "Yessir, wonder how much complainin' they woulda done then," he added. Soon Walter would be doing a little grumbling himself, though not because of the new size of our tow.

"Damn!" Walter cursed a few minutes later. "First Sunday paper I take time out to read in I don't know how long"—he kept rummaging through the pages—"and it don't

Mate Walter Otis Carroll shows us how soochin' should be done. He learned on old steamers.

have 'Snuffy Smith' or 'B.C.' Best two funnies there is," he declared, "and this paper don't have 'em. I gotta good mind to write this paper a letter," he said stuffed that week's *Des Moines Sunday Register* into a waste basket, and stormed out of the pilothouse.

"Walter's getting Channel Fever," Captain Hanks told me. "Most likely he's gone to shave off his beard right now. Always does that when he starts thinking about home," he laughed, "because his wife won't let him in the house with it."

Walter would be clean-shaven at the evening meal that night, and very quiet. He would be eating in the *Harriet M's* kitchen, but his thoughts would be with his family in Mt. Vernon, Indiana.

Twenty-five miles below Davenport, Walter and his crew caught the first double lockage—and the first rain since leaving St. Paul five days before—at Lock and Dam Number 16, at Muscatine, Iowa. This small river city, like so many others along the banks of the Upper Mississippi, began as an important lumbering point, then grew with the harvest and export of farm products grown in the fertile lands behind it.

At one time, however, Muscatine had a distinction all its own. For more than fifty years it was known as the "Button Capital of the World." It was the best and most prolific producer of mother-of-pearl buttons, fashioned by its factories from the shells of mussels living in the Mississippi's mud. But after World War II, when plastic buttons began to dominate the world's clothing fashions, the title was gone, and the last pearl button to be made in the world was polished and packed in the late 1960's for no delivery at all.

Today, Muscatine's few remaining button factories turn out the cheaper, plastic variety. But the little city still has a warehouse or two loaded with more than a million mother-of-pearls just waiting for the day America's nostalgia boom might bring them back into demand. Not a single mother-of-pearl is made anywhere else in the world today.

With our tow reassembled, we began to ease out of the lock. Larry Beale, a deckhand a long way from his home state of Maine, came into the pilothouse, shook the rain from his coat, and with a towel wiped his face and rain-soaked hair.

"I don't know what those people find so interesting about towboats that they'll stand out in the rain to watch us," he said, nodding toward the tourists. Tourists had been waving and shooting pictures of us at most of the locks we'd made during daylight hours. Today there was only one family, along with their dog, braving the rain to watch us make the lockage.

"With them watching us, and taking our pictures and all, I feel just like a monkey in a cage sometimes," Larry complained. "I'd sure like to get a camera and take their picture sometime—see how they like it," he wished out loud. I immediately sought the protection of the radar platform and began snapping pictures of the tourists. The men still on the barges began to cheer, whoop and hollar when a woman, one of the tourists who had caught me taking pictures of them, must have felt somewhat embarrassed and tried to hide behind a lifesaver station.

Inside the pilothouse, Captain Hanks was wearing a broad grin. "You just brought the morale up two hundred points," he said. "I've thought about doing that myself sometime, but I just never bothered bringing a camera from home." He laughed and looked toward the smiling deckhand from Maine. "Larry, fix this honorary riverman a cup of coffee," he said.

I suddenly felt very much at home.

A final torrent of rain beat against the pilot-house windows, then ended almost as quickly as it had begun.

With the sun and clear skies came the houseboats and the crestliners, the water-skiers and the fishermen. On the shores of islands or on the banks stretching below the rolling hills, campers and picknickers basked in the hot sun, fished from the banks, or sat by open cooking fires. There were countless passings of pleasure craft, and the deckhands often looked up from their work and waved to the girls sun bathing on the decks of many of the passing inboards.

Usually the girls lifted their heads to the men's "howdy there, honey," smiled and waved. Once, when we were slowly passing an island below the mouth of the Iowa River, four young women waved enthusiastically from the shore of the island—with the tops of their two-piece bathing suits! There was only one pair of binoculars on board—in the pilothouse. No one appeared on deck for five minutes. Talk about Channel Fever!

Under azure skies we moved steadily beyond Lock and Dam Number 18—and the four hills of Burlington, Iowa, a city that spreads itself down from the bluffs to the river's edge. The Mississippi here broadens between forested banks, its twisting current turning back off the shores of a number of islands. Beyond one of the larger of these, the channel carried us past the mouth of the Skunk River, which drools weakly from the Iowa bank into the Mississippi. Soon we were negotiating the Fort Madison bridge, whose span links Niota, Illinois, with Fort Madison. Here stood the first military outpost west of the Mississippi, now an important commercial, rail, and industrial center.

Some ten miles south, near the east bank of a quiet bend in the river, we came within sight of the small town of Nauvoo, Illinois, an agricultural community with its population today numbering less than two thousand. But at its peak, in 1845, Nauvoo had some 20,000 residents and was the largest city in the state. But it was one of the most ill-fated in American history. For it was here that thousands of Mormons (Church of Jesus Christ of Latter-day Saints) prospered, suffered, killed, or died in the face of religious persecution before they marched 1,500 miles to the "promised land" of Utah.

This epic march was the largest single migration in the history of the United States, but it was not the first time Mormons had to change their beliefs to flee. Within one year after he had founded the controversial religion, Joseph Smith and his followers, in 1831, were forced to leave their first church, at Fayette, New York. The Saints then set up headquarters in Kirkland, Ohio, and, with their belief that all non-Mormons were pagans, began working to recruit pagans. But stiff opposition to their revelations put them on the trail once again, which led them this time to Independence, Missouri, where their "ideal community" prospered until 1839, when irate orthodox protestants harried them out of the city.

It was in the spring of that year that Smith brought his followers to the small, six-building wilderness community of Commerce. He quickly renamed the site Nauvoo, "beautiful place," a name he derived from the Hebrew, and within five years the marshy wilderness became a progressive city with well laid-out streets, several manufacturing establishments, a fine hotel, and even a college.

By 1844 the Mormons' wealth had also given them strong

political power, the right to pass their own laws, to have their own city court—and to maintain their own militia. The Gentiles, as the non-Mormons were called, began to fear the Saints' power; and when Joseph Smith and his brother Hyrum were arrested for smashing the press of a few Mormon dissenters, an angry mob stormed the jail at Carthage and shot the brothers to death. Brigham Young took over Mormon leadership then and tried to achieve peace, but bitter armed clashes between the Gentiles and the Nauvoo Legion soon ended his peace-making. The Gentiles wanted the Mormons out of town, and after a bloody summer of 1846, Brigham Young agreed to take his people elsewhere. In the dead of winter, with little compensation for their property, five thousand men, women and children followed their new leader to the Great Salt Lake Basin, where they and the scores of Saints to follow survived the last of their persecutors.

Three years later French Icarians moved into the houses the Mormons had left behind. Under the leadership of Etienne Cabet, who had been expelled from France because of his socialist-utopian ideas, the Icarians set up their communistic workshops, labor gangs, community dining hall, and schools whose students were allowed to visit with their parents on Sundays only. Prosperity was theirs for several years. But in time a poor harvest, dissension among the workers, and individualism—the backbone of the American idea—destroyed Cabet's utopia. Nauvoo was again left to itself, to the land, and to the river.

In the prime of Mormon influence, Nauvoo had both progress and religion, but almost directly across the river lay a town not so interested in prosperity or temporal and spiritual salvation. In the 1840's Montrose was a ramshackle Iowa rivertown whose raw wood buildings stood ungraciously in contrast to the limestone and brick houses on the east bank; and that stretch of its front street facing the river was known from St. Paul to New Orleans as Rat Row, complete with saloons and rodents.

More than architecture, rats, and the mighty river separated these towns, however. While the Mormons tasted no tobacco or liquor—a fact which some say explains why Mormons have a lower death rate than that of any other group of people of the same size anywhere in the world—the men of Montrose lived with the free flow of their own brand of "spirits." Both booze and justice, it was said of the town, were administered by the same man over the same barrel of whisky.

But Montrose, one of the oldest white settlements in Iowa, was an important town on the Mississippi during the days of steam. For here lived the special rapids pilots who would take the giant packetboats down the treacherous, fifteen-mile Des Moines rapids to Keokuk.

The rapids are gone now, and the only troubled waters were those turned up in our wake as we made an easy approach for a single lockage at Keokuk, which has always been an important Mississippi city. In the golden days of steam, the city's levees were touched every year by no less than a thousand steamboats, and today its giant hydroelectric plant pours out power for cities as large and as distant as St. Louis.

But that day Keokuk had for me a special meaning. It was here that Samuel Langhorne Clemens (Mark Twain), after having worked as a tramp printer in St. Louis, New York, and Philadelphia, worked for a short time in his brother's print shop. From there, in 1857, he went to Cincinnati "and took passage on an ancient tub called the *Paul Jones*, for New Orleans," where he expected to board a steamer for South America, and the adventure and glory of exploring the headwaters of the Amazon. But another river, the Mississippi, claimed him instead.

Before he reached New Orleans, Samuel Clemens decided he wanted to become one of the "only unfettered and entirely independent human being(s) that lived in the earth," a river pilot, and he managed to convince Horace Bixby, a pilot on the *Paul Jones*, to take him on as a cub. For nearly a year and a half, he traveled and studied twelve hundred miles of the Mississippi. Then, as was permitted in those days, he began piloting without a license steamboats that carried only cargo. But in 1859, "The inspectors for the district of St. Louis certify that Samuel Clemens, having been duly examined, touching his qualifications as *PILOT* of a Steam Boat, is a suitable and safe person to be entrusted with the powers and duties of a Pilot of Steam Boats, and do license him to act as such for one year from this date on the following rivers, to wit on the Mississippi River to and from St. Louis and New Orleans."

For Sam Clemens, his years as a pilot were the happiest of his life, as he often admitted in later years. He might have remained a riverman, too, had not the Civil War intervened in 1861, when Louisiana seceded from the Union. Sam Clemens lost his last command at the New Orleans dock. There his boat was seized in the Confederacy's name—still unofficial at the time.

Beyond the mouth of the Des Moines River, the borderline between Iowa and Missouri, we plied a gentle channel past the small-town levees of Warsaw, Canton, and La Grange, from where small boys, each one perhaps with his own dream of becoming a river pilot, still wave to the passing boats. Then, several miles south of the bluff where the site of a Sauk Indian Village has become the industrialized trade center of Quincy, Illinois, the channel buoys directed the *Harriet M* safely beyond Turtle Island and into Mark Twain's boyhood Mississippi. Hannibal, Missouri, is the "St. Petersberg" of *Tom Sawyer*.

Hannibal consisted of nothing more elaborate than a few log cabins and a trading post in the early nineteenth century. But by the time Mark Twain left Hannibal, in 1853, it was an important town on the Mississippi, exporting its share of grain, tobacco, livestock. The town also mined coal, quarried limestone, and sawed the log rafts brought downriver from Wisconsin and Minnesota. Later it became an important rail center, with more than fifty passenger trains stop-ping there daily.

Although only freights stop there today, Hannibal still maintains itself as a small industrial town on the river, and it has not forgotten its favorite son. Some of its Mark Twain nostalgia is gawdy, with painted and neon signs advertising hotels, restaurants, and shopping centers named after just about every character you can think of in Mark Twain's fiction. But at the foot of Cardiff Hill stands the bronze statue of the two adventurous boys, Tom Sawyer and Huckelberry Finn. Each year Tom's mischievous spirit is relived when real boys splash themselves and Tom's fence with a fresh coat of whitewash. And there still stands the little house where the boy Mark Twain lived and played and dreamed until the age of eighteen, when he left Hannibal to see the world and to become a universally loved American writer.

After he had quit Hannibal for good, never to live there again, Mark Twain made several return visits to relatives and friends in the town. One such visit took place on a Sunday morning, twenty-nine years after he had left those cobblestone streets.

"The things about me and before me," Twain remembered that day in *Life on the Mississippi*, "made me feel like a boy again—convinced me that I was a boy again, and that I had simply been dreaming an unusually long dream." These were his thoughts while he stood on the height of Holiday Hill, where—"From this vantage-ground the extensive view up and down the river, and wide over the wooded expanse of Illinois, is very beautiful—one of the most beautiful on the Mississippi, I think."

The river and the country here is still beautiful, and that day I wanted to see it all, be as close to it as I could. For hours I sat Indian-fashion near the head of the lead barges, hundreds of yards beyond the thundering of the *Harriet M's* engines. Here the only sound was the hissing of the river being pushed aside by the flat, steel heads of the barges as we slowly sailed down Mark Twain's beloved Mississippi.

The last bold bluffs and Huck's "mountains on the Missouri shore" slipped behind us a few miles south of Hannibal, and the riverbanks now became flatter and densely forested with willows and birches and cottonwoods. A medley of birdsong came from the banks, and flocks of swallows would leap now and then into the air, circle the treetops, and fly quickly across our bow. There was peace and reflection here for me, as every mile of this stretch of the Mississippi echoes those adventurous days of Tom Sawyer. I, too, felt like a boy again, especially when we entered that part of the channel that flows safely to the right of a particular island below Saverton, Missouri.

"Three miles below St. Petersberg, at a point where the Mississippi River was a trifle over a mile wide," Twain enchants us in *The Adventures of Tom Sawyer*, "there was a long, narrow, wooded island, with a shallow bar at the head of it, and this offered well as a rendezvous. It was not inhabited, it lay far over toward the further shore, abreast a dense and almost wholly unpeopled forest. So Jackson's Island was chosen."

With its shores at the mercy of an unpredictable river, Jackson's Island has changed somewhat since Mark Twain wrote about it. There never was a "tolerable long, steep hill or ridge about forty feet high" near the cavern in which Huck and Jim slept out the storm. But in the misty dusk I thought for a moment that I saw shadows, the shadows of Tom Sawyer, the Black Avenger of the Spanish Main; Huck Finn the Red-Headed; and Joe Harper the terror of the Seas as "The raft drew beyond the middle of the river; the boys pointed her head right, and then lay on their oars."

Just north of the harsh but short-lived cliffs of Cap Au Gris, Missouri, the site of Lock and Dam Number 25, fog once again closed the channel, forcing us to tie off at the bank for several hours. Though the river's channel was clear, the radio channels were crowded with both business and stern-line talk of the pilots and captains of other towboats that had tied off at the west bank north and south of us. When the fog lifted the next morning I saw a string of tows lined up behind us.

Captain Hanks studied the line of tows, some of which were already beginning to move away from the bank. "It's going to be a race to this lock," Captain Hanks said, "but we got them beat." He switched on the intercom. "Get those lines off, Walter. We got two loads coming up behind." He then called Willie Anderson, our chief engineer. "Get those diesels working, and quick," he yelled.

Within a few minutes the bank-side river boiled up behind us, and we headed into the channel, five hundred yards ahead of the first of a half dozen other southbound tows.

"There's only two more locks after this one," Captain Hanks told me as he got the tow in shape for its approach to Lock Number 25. "But we could end up waiting a couple of days before we can get through the one at Alton."

Lock and Dam Number 26, at Alton, Illinois, is at a critical navigational point on the Upper Mississippi. It is only ten miles south of the mouth of the Illinois River, a heavily traveled commercial waterway, and immediately north of where the Missouri, also a towboat river, enters the Mississippi. Any tows moving south out of the Illinois or from the Upper Mississippi have to lock through Alton; and any boats traveling upstream from the river north of St. Louis or from the Missouri must also lock there.

For the Alton lock is the sole waterway connection between the Upper Mississippi Basin and the continental interior to the south, with the Mississippi and its tributaries bringing products to and from such diversified river ports as Pittsburgh on the east; Sioux City on the west; and the Gulf Coast, directly south.

"There's so many boats using that lock," Captain Hanks complained, "that I've had to wait as long as three days before I could get through."

The captain also told me that the Army Corps of Engineers has plans to relieve the bottleneck with two 1200-foot locks it would like to build two miles downstream

Captain Kenny Hanks takes a break from his cigarettes and coffee to relax and enjoy a pipe of home-blended tobacco.

of Alton. Plans for the locks' construction were approved by the Secretary of the Army in 1969, but ecologists opposing any new construction on that part of the river have managed to delay the project, claiming that the two additional miles of pool that would be created by the proposed locks would cause drastic ecological damage to the river and its wildlife.

"I don't mind the ecology people wanting to get the river clean again," Captain Hanks admitted. "I'd kind of like to see clean water and blue skies all over the world, but I know enough that it can't be done overnight, and that you just can't bring commerce to a dead stop to do it. And what I really don't like about it all," he declared, "is that those ecology people are stopping the new locks with railroad money."

Again enters the hostility between rivermen and railroad men. The towboat companies, of course, are backing the construction of the new locks, arguing that unless the locks are built, the river's commerce will be restrained to its present level, which, by the way, is very impressive. The Mississippi and its navigable tributaries from Alton to Minneapolis, plus the Illinois to Chicago, transported seventy millions tons of cargo in 1973. More than half of this was locked through at Alton.

On the other hand, the railroads say they are concerned that a more efficient commercial Mississippi will "have catastrophic effects on the plaintiff railroads and on the communities served by these railroads." Thus stated a suit filed by twenty-one rail companies in 1974.

The court battle continues (as of this writing, an October 23, 1979, decision allowing a new lock is in appeal), and the towboats still wait. But that day we entered the lock after only a minor delay. Captain Hanks was especially happy about that. He left the *Harriet M* here and was home with his family that night.

Buddy Howell moved into the Captain's position and would now work the more favored six-to-twelve shift, and our new relief pilot, Shelden A. DeTrafford, a young lanky Cajun from Baton Rouge, would take the graveyard shift.

Buddy guided the *Harriet M* beyond the mouth of the "Big Muddy" Missouri River to a point just north of an obstructing reach known as the Chain of Rocks. Then, after several hours delay that brought us into late evening, we passed through the final lock (its chamber was undergoing repairs and had to be double-locked) and then the ten-mile, man-made Chain of Rocks Canal.

Under clear midnight skies, Shelden worked the rudder levers as we moved out of the canal and entered St. Louis's Mississippi. From where I stood on the *Harriet M's* Texas deck, the immediate riverbanks were dark, and only occasionally lights from factories or warehouses cast a dim reflection over the river. But the city itself was a grand display of lights, and a bright sky gave a stunning view of the Eads Bridge, an engineering marvel of the nineteenth century. It was from this bridge that I'd first seen the Mississippi twenty years before, and had my first thoughts of someday sailing down the mighty river that "goes all the way to the ocean, son."

Most people said this bridge could not be built at St. Louis, where the turbulent river reached one of its widest points. But James Buchannan Eads, the same man who had provided the Union with seven ironclad gunboats within sixty-four days, said he could and would build such a bridge. In July of 1867 Eads' newly formed bridge company began construction, and after nearly ten million dollars, seven years of engineering difficulties, construction deaths, and floods, the more-than-a-mile long bridge was dedicated on July 4, 1874. It opened to both highway and rail traffic, for Eads had made this first bridge to cross the river at St. Louis a two-level span, with the upper level for wagons and the lower for trains.

As we came out from under the Eads Bridge, which is still in use today, I could see Eero Saarinen's 620-foot "Gateway Arch," reflecting city lights and gleaming like a spectral rainbow near the river's edge. It was near here, in 1764, that Auguste Chouteau and his men worked under the commandership of Pierre Laclede and built the trading post of St. Louis, where Indians gathered once a year to exchange their furs for the white man's blankets, firearms and firewater.

From this modest beginning Laclede said he "intended to establish a settlement which might hereafter become one of the finest cities in America," and within five years his city became and remained the center of Western fur trade. After the Louisiana Purchase in 1803 transferred St. Louis and all the Louisiana territory to the United States, more and more goods, supplies, and people began to find their way to and from the Mississippi's central city. By 1860 the riverport became one of the busiest in the world, with thousands of steamboats calling there each year.

Today, the St. Louis riverfront stretches some twenty miles along the river. On the bank are miles of factories and warehouses; and on the river are dozens of landing fleets lining the banks, where scores of barges load tons of grain, coal, sand, chemicals; or empty their wells of steel, cement, minerals, petroleum products. More than three thousand manufacturers supply the world's market with products ranging from bullets to stoves, caskets to railroad cars—and beer, with the Anheuser-Busch plant here pouring out some seven million gallons of foaming brew each year.

To help make next year's brew, Herbie and Big John from Texas, the assistant tankerman, began their part: the twelve-hour pumping-off operation, opening or closing giant valves and checking guages. They watched the barge's temperature closely as the molasses that would feed the yeast to make the beer Buddy, Shelden and I were going to drink when we got our time off flowed steadily into the bank-born storage tanks.

Working on a molasses barge is hot and dirty work. When Herbie came into the pilothouse that night for a cold drink of water he "looked and smelled like a pancake that had fallen into the river," as Shelden put it.

"Well, I don't know 'bout you." Herbie said after he had taken a long, cool drink, "but I believe in that reincarnation stuff. And when I get finished makin' brew with the devil and the boys, I want to come back as a coonass pilot"—coonass is a riverman's 'affectionate' term for a Cajun—"or an easy livin' book-writer."

"Well. . .I don't know what to come back as," Shelden said slowly. "I guess I'd have to come back as Socks, my wife's dog," he decided. "Damn dog won't eat 'less its fed a TV dinner, and that's gotta be served on a TV tray with the TV turned on. And he gets his way all the time 'cause we don't have any kids—except him."

Naturally I asked the right question: What kind of dog did his wife have?

"Well. . .I don't have any papers for him but I got proof that he's a pure-blooded, pedigreed 'Smart-Dog'."

Thre three of us laughed. Then this "easy-livin' book-writer" went to his room and wrote it all down.

CHAPTER SEVEN

BRIDGES, FIRE AND DEATH

Flies! Black Flies, Blowflies, Botflies, Green-bottle Flies, Stone-Flies, and flies maybe never catalogued by science could be found day or night in the pilothouse. Sometimes only one or two would make the rounds between arms, legs, cheeks, and coffee cups; and sometimes whole gangs of them would flurry crazily through the air, buzzing from one end of the pilothouse to the other. To Captain Hanks, flies are just a part of working on the river, and he'd never once complained about them. Only when one or two might have made a three-point landing on the brim of his coffee cup had he bothered to notice them, wave them away with a slow, casual brush of his hand.

Shelden, too, seems to accept the flies as just part of working on the river. But not Buddy; he hates flies, and he always keeps a fly swatter within easy reach. While I spent time in the pilothouse during Buddy's watches, it was a common occurrence (one that took me several days to accept without flinching) for him to suddenly snatch the fly swatter, jump from the pilot's chair, and swing wildly at the pests as they raced about the pilothouse. He cursed them during the entire course of his attacks, and he usually ordered a deckhand to "get up here with more flypaper," which he then hung lavishly near the doors and windows. At night, when I might be sitting near the head of the tow or watching the river roll away from our stern, the pilothouse lights behind me would suddenly flash on and I'd see Buddy—head raised, his arm working the fly swatter on all eight cylinders—chasing after the flies.

Buddy was in the middle of some fly-chasing when I went to the pilothouse late the next morning. My equipment was packed and on deck, and I was getting ready to leave. The molasses had been pumped off, and the *Harriet M* would be leaving St. Louis in a few hours. I had had no word as to another ride, and I wanted to say good-bye before going to the bank and trying for another southbound hitch.

"These are river-flies," Buddy said. "They work six on and six off, seven days a week"—he made a few fast swings—"and they always get on my watch!"

I told Buddy that if he could stop killing flies long enough, I would like to have a last cup of coffee with him before I left. Buddy raised his fly swatter at me, laughed, then lowered it, sat in the pilot's chair, and leaned back and rested his feet on the control panel.

"Who said anything about killing those river-flies? I was just trying to train them, get them in shape so's they could help you unpack all your clothes and those fancy cameras you're always carrying around." He looked directly at me then and started laughing. "How do you like that! I forgot to tell you that we're going all the way to New Orleans and you can go right on down with us, if you still want to."

When Buddy was finished laughing at his little joke, and before I would carry all my equipment back to my quarters and unpack everything, I told him that he was having so much trouble with flies because he wasn't using the fly swatter properly. All the action has to be in the wrist. I would show him how it was done in New Jersey, I told him. Buddy stood and handed me the fly swatter. I tested its swing, then told the pilot that he would have to look toward the bank, either one, and watch for stars.

"Stars?" he asked, but before he could turn around I landed one fly swatter on one tail of one hell of a riverman.

Late that afternoon, with the aid of a small harbor tow, Shelden maneuvered the *Harriet M* out of the dangerously low water near the west bank and brought her safely around and into the channel of this heavily industrialized stretch of the Mississippi. The St. Louis river bank is crowded with factories, warehouses, storage tanks, and loading docks. Directly across from St. Louis, mills, factories, warehouses, and railroad yards stand above the river on the levees of East St. Louis, Illinois. It is the largest city on the vast Mississippi flood plain known as the American Bottom.

Beneath a portion of these levees is the land of what was once a mile-long sandbar known as Bloody Island. The sandbar is one with the land now, with freight yards and warehouses, but in the early nineteenth century dense willows and cottonwoods made it a perfect shelter for the more lusty hearted of the town. Within easy reach of the bank, Bloody Island became their favorite arena for illegal boxing bouts, cock fights, and duels, the last fatality giving the island its name. In August 1831, Major Thomas Biddle and Spencer Pettis, a member of the 21st Congress, chose pistols, stood only five feet apart, then shot each other to death.

Several miles to the south stands Cahokia, Illinois' oldest town. There are nearly a hundred mounds of the mysterious river-dwellers of the Mississipian culture still in tact, but the town itself is all but lost in the smoky and virile industry of East St. Louis.

Once she was in the channel, her whistle blasting during passages, the *Harriet M* became part of a hectic and noisy river highway busy with north and southbound traffic: switch boats, tugboats, excursion boats, pleasure craft, and other tows. To a layman like myself it was a floating mayhem. But to Sheldon it was just another southbound run through the St. Louis port, and he casually but expertly guided our tow of seven empty barges beyond the trees and buildings of Jefferson Barracks, the first United States Army training-school, and out of the confines of brick and steel, smoke and soot.

Though there are the industrial reminders of an occasional landing fleet or dock, the river below St. Louis generally flows between a pleasant countryside, a natural-beauty wilderness of ever-changing character. Looking east or west, I would see thickly wooded cliffs, horizon-bound flatlands, rocky hills, and trees—great stretches of unbroken forests, between all of which would be a lone house or a hamlet or a small city.

The last of the river's locks and dams—and the delays that usually go with them—were behind us now, and through that day and evening we sailed steadily past numerous towns and cities. Prairie du Rocher, Illinois, a somnolent little town that was founded as a result of John Law's "Mississippi Bubble," a financial scheme that, when it burst in 1720, almost wrecked the French economy. Further downstream lies St. Genevive, Missouri, the gay French town whose old St. Genevive Savings Bank was once robbed by Jesse James. Later we sailed past Kaskaskia Island, the only section of Illinois that lies west of the Mississippi, and Rockwood, whose rich Illinois timberlands supplied fuel for thousands of steamers as well as supplied the lumber for many a flatbottomed boat that would carry rich cargos down the river in its early days of commerce.

The next day, 150 miles south of St. Louis, just 30 miles above the confluence of the Ohio and Mississippi rivers, we passed the old waterfront houses of Cape Girardeau, Missouri. It's here that the river's famous levees, fifteen to forty feet high, begin to stretch southward for more than 1,500 miles to a point below New Orleans, a length greater than that of the Great Wall of China.

And at dusk of my ninth day aboard the *Harriet M*, my seventeenth day hitching the Mississippi, I stood outside the pilothouse and looked to where the wooded east bank is part of a massive earthen levee that extends southward along the most southern end of Illinois, then rounds the tip of this peninsula and travels up the west bank of the Ohio River. Behind this levee and a cement floodwall stands the city of Cairo, its east bank washed by the Ohio and its west bank ending at the final stretch of the Upper Mississippi.

Located on the confluence of two great American rivers, Cairo had the promise of becoming the commercial capitol of the Middle West. But the town had a late start and early in the Civil War its north-south trade routes were closed. The Union was quick to recognize Cairo's strategic location, and within six months after shots were traded at Fort Sumter, Ulysses S. Grant set up headquarters in the town and turned the town into a concentration point for his armies and the base for a gunboats of his Western Flotilla, later renamed the Mississippi Squadron. The early success of these gunboats on the Tennessee and Cumberland rivers brought more than twelve thousand Confederate prisoners to the city to await their transport to northern prisons. Later, after the fall of Vicksburg, some thirty thousand more would follow.

Like so many other river towns, Cairo found its river commerce rejuvenated after the war. More than eight thousand people lived among the city's canebrakes and the cottonfields, ginko and magnolia trees when the war had ended, and by 1867 thousands of steamboats again called at her levee. But soon the tracks of as many as seven railroads found their way into the city, and Cairo's river-dependent prosperity dwindled, never to return. The scores of towboats calling there today stay only long enough to break or assemble tows at the number of landing fleets anchored at the city's east bank, several miles up the Ohio River.

As we sailed past this most southern tip of America's "Egypt," I watched the slow-moving, blue-gray torrent of the Ohio River mix with the greenish-yellow waters of the Mississippi, the waters of both great streams tumbling together with a rainbow-like sparkle in the day's last light. Ever darkening was the sky. The sky, the land and the rivers were darkening, but I could still appreciate the awesomeness of the Ohio. For here the Mississippi, a giant in its own right, is only half as wide as the Ohio at its mouth. At this confluence, the Ohio feeds the Father of Waters with almost twice as much water as the mighty river brings down from all its northern tributaries. And it was out of this mouth that the first steamboat came to challenge and ride the back of the Mississippi.

More than a hundred and fifty years ago, in the autumn of 1811, Nicholas Roosevelt, ancestor of the presidents, sailed the 116-foot-long side-wheeler *New Orleans* out of Pittsburgh and steamed down the Ohio River, determined to reach the levees of the Crescent City. News of the little steamer's challenge to the great rivers traveled up and down the Ohio and Mississippi, but though talk of the *New Orleans* stirred up excitement, many said, "It's easy enough for a steamboat to go down the river, but it will never get back up against the current." So the confident Roosevelt told his captain, Henry M. Shreve, who knew the river as a seasoned keel-boatman, to stop at a number of river ports on the Ohio to take on passengers for a short upstream ride before returning them safely to the bank. By the time Roosevelt was ready to bring his steamboat into the Mississippi, he was sure and proud of the *New Orleans'* power.

But the Mississippi was proud—and powerful—as well. When the *New Orleans* was well into her maiden voyage, the mighty river spit wildly at its first taste of steam. The first of nearly two thousand tremors of the New Madrid earthquake began to hammer and break the earth on the banks and beneath the river. Exploding into giant fountains and geysers, the angry Mississippi broke and drowned familiar islands—including one that the *New Orleans* had tied up to one night. The angry river threw new lands above its surface; and it splintered scores of rafts, flatboats, and keelboats that had been caught unaware in what may have been the greatest series of earthquakes (tremors continued for two years) to hit the North American continent since recorded history. The river tore and destroyed its own banks, sweeping New Madrid and Little Prairie—now Caruthersville, Missouri—into its waters and washing them down to the sea. Turning on itself time and again, the river even changed its course and traveled strongly northward for several hours that December day, washing over the Tennessee bank and filling a giant depression in the land that is today the 18-mile long Reelfoot Lake.

The river had twisted and turned in all directions, raised and lowered itself, but when its storm of violence had cleared the little steamboat was still there, destined to reach New Orleans and cheering crowds in January of 1812. But the river still had its current, and the *New Orleans*, being no match for it, could strain no further north than Natchez. She was put into service on the first steam-traveled New Orleans-Natchez run, carrying both passengers and cargo until 1814. The river claimed its first steamboat with a snag shrewdly hidden beneath its surface.

The *New Orleans'* small but impressive victory over the river, however, proved that steam-travel was possible on America's western waterways; and so began—after more trial and error—the Mississippi's most glorious period. Daniel French, already experimenting with steam on the Ohio, was eager to have a boat make the south-north trip on the Mississippi, and in 1814, sent his *Comet* to conquer the river. The little side-wheeler made the voyage to New Orleans, but like the *New Orleans*, she could not push further north than Natchez. French eventually had her dismantled and sent another challenger, the *Vesuvius*, only to have her fall to the same end. Then, in 1815, French's *Enterprise*, under the commandership of Shreve, who had run the 75-ton steamer through the British blockade during the Battle of New Orleans the year before, made the long journey up the Mississippi and the Ohio to Louisville, Kentucky. Eventually she docked at the river port of Pittsburgh.

Five years after he served as captain aboard the first steam-powered boat to work the Mississippi, Henry Shreve decided he would put his hard-earned knowledge to work for himself, and he built his first steamboat, the 400-ton *Washington*. She was the first steamboat to have a shallow-draft hull, one that enabled her to sit on the water rather than sink into it; the first truly high-pressure engines, the boilers standing horizontally rather than vertically; and, with a boxlike pilothouse sitting high between the engines' two chimneys, she was the first double-decked steamer to sail the river. The *Washington* could make the current as well and became the true mother of the Mississippi steamboat.

Bigger and faster steamboats followed the *Washington*, and the Age of Steam was in full bloom by the mid-nineteenth century. Tourists, settlers and gamblers traveled in the luxury of the floating palaces, and the towns they settled in or visited, flourished with the new economic boom brought to the Ohio and Mississippi valleys by steam. By 1860 there were nearly a thousand steamers calling at the ports of Cincinnati, St. Louis, Natchez, and New Orleans. There seemed to be no end to the growth of commerce on the river, and no limit to the growth of the country because of it.

Then came the Civil War and the fast-improving, all-year-running railroads, safe and swift compared to the steamboat. By the turn of the century, only a few steamers were working on America's rivers, and these were barely surviving.

When America faced another war, in 1917, it gave new life to the Mississippi. World War I found the nation's railroads incapable of moving all its needs for the war "over there," so the government turned to America's natural highways, to its rivers, particularly the Mississippi and its seaward course. The War Department quickly put into service every steamboat and pilot it could find, loading the decks of the steamers with the sorely needed supplies of war. When the war ended, Americans realized the river and the steamboats had served them well. The nation would never leave them barren again, though the steamboats would eventually give way to the more modern and powerful diesel-powered boats of today.

Traveling aboard a steamboat on the Mississippi was certainly a luxurious and exciting affair, but it was also a dangerous one. By 1850 over five hundred steamboats and thousands of passengers had become casualties of collisions, fires, snags, rapids, sandbars, rocks and exploding boilers. Among the hundred people killed when four of the *Pennsylvania's* eight boilers blew was Mark Twain's own brother, Henry Clemens.

The average life of a steamer was no longer than five years, and it was reckoned—even accepted—that each one would come to a violent end within that time. But hardy passengers still filled the staterooms of the floating palaces.

Of course, the later boats sailing the Mississippi traveled a safer river after the government began to dredge the channel, remove snags and rocks, and calm the rapids. But the pilots were faced with a new, unremovable enemy, one that was multiplying as fast as the commerce on and near the navigable channels in the nation's inland waterway system—the bridge. Scores of boats, both steamer and diesel, lost control in the river's swift current and slammed into and sank beside the bridge piers. Even today pilots feel that the bridge is more dangerous than anything the river itself might threaten.

No bridge is taken lightly by the modern towboat pilot. Each one sweats a little and brings his senses to peak awareness when his tow approaches the menacing piers of a highway or railroad bridge. For within seconds a changing current or a sudden shift in the wind, even on the calmer and carefully regulated inland channels, can mean death and destruction.

On the night of September 13, 1970, for instance, Captain Buddy Howell was at the controls of the towboat *Delta Cities*, moving four gasoline-filled tank barges through the Sabine-Naches Canal and headed towards Baton Rouge, Louisiana. As he steered for the channel running beneath the West Port

Arthur Bridge, the captain saw that his tow was in good shape and began to guide it between the bridge's piers.

Everything looked good; the tow was well out into the canal and still in fine shape. Just another routine passing. But then the tow began to shift. The afterend of the last barge began to slide slowly towards the steel walling of the bridge's right fender. Buddy, alone in the pilothouse, pulled hard at the rudder. Only a few more feet and that last barge would be clear. But the bridge seemed to draw the tow like a magnet.

Then there was the agonizing cry of steel ripping steel. The contact between barge and bridge had only been momentary, but time enough for part of the steel walling to gash the barge's stern. Gasoline began to escape and immediately ignited. Within seconds the *Delta Cities* was engulfed by flames; the channel was a consuming torrent; and the bridge was burning as well.

Buddy hit the towboat's general alarm. Its bell clanged frighteningly as all hands dropped cups of coffee, or pen and paper, or stumbled from their bunks to abandon their dying boat. The whistle blasted and blasted and blasted, warning the tankers loading at the Texaco refineries dead ahead.

Every foot of the *Delta Cities* was burning, but Buddy stayed in the pilothouse. He continued to sound the alarm, stay at the controls, work feverishly to maneuver the listing and burning tow safely away from the tankers and refineries ahead. Miraculously, he managed to get the burning tow against the far bank of Pleasure Island, make a room to room search for his men, and then leap over the side and into the flaming water.

"Arriving at the scene a few minutes after the accident and seeing the fire on the *Delta Cities*, bridge, and surrounding waters," wrote H. E. Priddy, Captain of the tug

Havoline, "I was astonished to see that this tow was taken so far from the scene of the accident before the *Delta Cities* was abandoned by Captain Howell.

"Mr. Larry King, Relief Mate on the *SS Texaco Wyoming*, and his crew relate they thought for a few seconds that their vessel would be rammed. Their attention was attracted by the continuous signal being sounded from the tow...they could see Captain Howell through the flames, still at the wheel, trying to get it away from the island."

Buddy was given a commendation for his bravery that evening. But awards, as fine a thing as they are, can never erase memories of death. Three of Buddy's men died that night. One of them, a young deckhand Buddy had often brought home with him, had been like a second son to the captain and his wife. A piece of Buddy had died along with those men, and it was years before a different kind of courage brought him back to his friends and family, to the boats, and to the river.

At that point where the waters of the Ohio are finally mixed with those of the Mississippi, the Upper Mississippi ends and the Lower Mississippi begins. It is here that a shoreline was eons ago, the northern edge of the Gulf of Mexico. But through the ages the river filled those waters with ton upon ton of silt and sediment; and today it flows nearly one thousand miles through the land of its own making, carrying to the present Gulf, waters that have tasted land as distant as those of Pennsylvania and Montana. Beginning here is the giant, unstoppable stream whose majesty earned it the Indian and Negro nicknames of Old Big Strong, Old Man River, and Old Devil River.

Unlike the upper river, which flows between the borders of natural walls, the lower river rides high, often higher than the land itself, twisting and turning through its geological delta, eating away at its own confines and at the earth that men have had to raise up against it. For there are times when the Father of Waters reaches out to reclaim the fertile land it has given, as it did in 1927, when it reached to millions of acres of land, spreading as much as eighty miles in some places, and driving more than 600,000 people from their homes.

Since then, under orders from Congress, the Army Corps of Engineers has been fighting hard to tame this giant, to force it to work only for man and not against him. But knowing that the river will someday rebel with a superflood that they will never be able to stop completely, the Engineers have made concessions to the river and built floodways between Cairo and New Madrid, which we sailed past that evening. They also built them in Atchafalaya Basin, completed as recently as 1965, and at Morganza above Baton Rouge, Louisiana. The lands here will be offered as a temporary sacrifice to the "river of the sky," and when the raging waters approach New Orleans, they will be allowed to race to the sea through the Bonnet Carre Spillway and Lake Pontchartrain.

Around-the-clock, crossings are dredged, banks are graded, and massive steel and concrete mats are assembled and laid to strengthen those ever-weakening banks to which the river shows no mercy. There can be no dams placed in the face of this river, for there are no places to anchor them, and any water backed up by a dam would swiftly drown the very flat land which the river fights to claim. So the Engineers have piled up more than 800,000,000 cubic yards of earth to protect land and lives along the river. But this Old Devil River seems to merely tolerate rather than accept the confines man has built for it. And in 1973 the river reminded the Engineers

River fighters: Men and machines work round the clock to keep the river back.

of its power, not giving a damn for their efforts, and smashed beyond the barriers to put seven million acres and over $160 million worth of property beneath its raging waters.

On the Lower Mississippi there are fewer towns and for Buddy and Sheldon this meant fewer bridges for them to negotiate, though there would be the dreaded piers at Greenville, Vicksburg, and New Orleans. And for the crew the swiftness of the new river and the absence of locks meant that we would make New Orleans in half the time it had taken us to sail the upper river.

The atmosphere of the river had certainly changed now, and so had the atmosphere aboard the *Harriet M*. Though not a single man had said anything about having a new lightheartedness on the lower river, I could sense the quiet celebration within each of them. There was more talk at meal time. The younger deckhands became livelier and more often engaged in friendly horseplay; they seemed to mind less the increased teasing of the older rivermen.

There was a new feeling aboard the *Harriet M*, and Buddy decided he would let everyone know his good spirits by coming up with a new "snow job," one that could be played only because I was aboard, and one in which I would have to take part if it was to be successful.

While we had been pumping off molasses in St. Louis, we had taken on an additional tankerman by the name of Ed Critchloe. When I met the new crewmember, he had made a pleasant first impression, and a very neat one, with his work clothes being absolutely spotless and sharply pressed. He was friendly and eager to talk. I was sure I'd get some good river stories from him when he came back from getting his gear stowed away and making his rounds in the tank barges. But when I saw him again, in the kitchen, started a conversation, he seemed nervous and couldn't wait to get out the back door.

I was in the pilothouse, listening to some old stories Shelden was glad to pass along to a new ear, when Buddy came in quickly, trying to balance a cup of coffee as he shook with laughter.

"Now I already told Ed that you're one of those efficiency experts that the company sent out here to find ways they can cut costs," Buddy said, and that explained the odd and nervous glances I got from the tankerman at the evening meal. "All you have to do is take his picture once in a while, look at your watch a little, then write something down." He handed me a clipboard and paper. "Just write down any crazy thing that comes into your head, some nutty way to save money on a towboat," he instructed. "Then leave it where Ed can take a look at it."

I frowned at the idea, and Buddy added, "Everyone is in on it and counting on you, even Emma." How could I refuse?

Soon I began getting calls from the men, telling me where Ed was at a particular time—on the barges, in the kitchen, with the engineer, in the pilothouse. I would go to where he was, look around, take his picture, scribble with my pen and leave. When I wasn't being sent after Ed, I sat and made up my "efficiency" notes. After the evening meal that night, I "absent-mindedly" left the clipboard with my notes on the counter, where anyone who might want to could sneak a look. I put the notes there, not too far from where Ed was sitting and watching me, and left for the pilothouse to join Shelden.

Following are some of my "time saving" observations and suggestions:

Men use up five seconds to scrape their dishes

after each meal, but another 6.5 seconds and they could rinse them.

TV dinners could be used to save on having a cook on board.

Walking across the tow is a big time loss. With shoes having suction-cupped heels and soles they could run.

Perhaps tankermen could sleep on tank barges, saving additional travel time to and from their bunks.

Shelden urinates in coffee can while piloting—big time-saver! *(This is true. Whenever he does this, Shelden shouts a warning to anyone who might be downwind, then tosses the waste overboard.)*

Tankermen like Ed Critchloe have free time and could help the cook wash the linen on Mondays. In fact, each crewmember could have a personalized laundry bag. These could be hung outside the crew's quarters for the tankermen to pick up. There might be some complaints in the beginning, but I feel certain that the deckhands will quickly adjust to having their underwear bleached by tankermen.

A few minutes later Buddy, Herbie, Walter and Arkansas Bill came to the pilothouse. They were laughing so hard that it was several minutes before they could tell Shelden and me what had happened.

"Ed didn't want any part of those notes at first," Buddy laughed. "But then Bill started him going, reading your notes and cursing."

"He still didn't want any part of them notes," Arkansas Bill picked up the story. "But I guess it was too much for him." Arkansas Bill started laughing. "Let me tell ya, son, he just eased his way over to the water cooler and started reading from the corner of his eye. But it wasn't a minute longer before he was leaning right over 'em. His eyes got bigger than searchlights; he turned redder than a coon's ass in a briar patch and ran outta there madder than hell. Didn't even finish his supper."

When I left the *Harriet M* in New Orleans, I was still an efficiency expert, as far as Ed was concerned; and, according to letters I have received from some of the men since then, no one has bothered to tell him otherwise as of this writing.

CHAPTER EIGHT

TO NEW ORLEANS AND THE SEA

It was quiet inside the pilothouse now. The laughter had gone to sleep with the shift change, and the eerie orange lights of the radarscope and the fathometer strengthened as the day ended in glorious battleflags of crimson and gold, indigo and purple. Buddy was quiet and reflective at the controls, barely moving his eyes from the river ahead of us as he sipped at his coffee, worked the rudder levers, and brought us around another bend. The bank to our right was still Missouri, but left was the willow-lined bank of Kentucky, Buddy's home state.

"I always get to thinking about home when the river starts getting dark," Buddy said finally. "I guess every man away from home does that about this time of day, but for me it's a special time. I know that my Mary Lee is thinking about me right this minute." The pilot clicked a switch, and the searchlights shot their beams onto the river, searching for the channel markers. "It's something we started more than twenty years ago," he told me, "and there hasn't been a single sunset when I've been on the river that we missed thinking about each other for a few minutes. It's a long wait before you get your time off, and doing something like that kind of helps. . ."

And for the towboat widows, the wives of the rivermen,

the wait is long as well.

"The only thing you can do is keep busy," a river wife says. "Those first years were the worst for me, but then the children started to come along—two boys and four girls in eleven years—and I had a lot to keep my mind occupied. But now three of them are married and the others are getting into their own way, wanting to do things for themselves. So now each day I try to save things to do during those hours when my husband would be home if he weren't working on the river. The longest days are Sundays, and that's when I do a lot of cleaning. The weekdays are the best; they're work days, and they're the days when the mailman comes and might bring me a letter."

Letters. From the river to the land and from the land to the river the letters travel day and night to keep a rendezvous, when they will talk of love and loneliness and the river. Or they might speak of everyday things at home—the kids, school, the washing machine needing to be repaired—or the routine of towboat days. They might be neatly typed and articulate explanations to a wife not yet accustomed to handling the bills, clumsily penned love notes, or ten-page diaries in which the pain is no more than an undertone. Some carry quarrels or forgiveness over hundreds of miles. Some seek money or a picture of the new baby. Some are like open wounds. But whatever their description, these letters are important, necessary to the survival of husband and wife, son and mother, and young lovers; necessary to the very life of the relationship. Letters are the life blood of the river people.

A young deckhand sits in the corner of the kitchen and writes a letter to his family. Three other men get a card game going with the cook, laughing and joking as they gamble for a favorite pie for tomorrow's dessert. The young deckhand keeps on writing. In South Bend, Indiana, in a small farmhouse, a seasoned river wife writes a letter to her husband, a mate on a Mississippi line-haul boat. She writes slowly and carefully, telling how well the farm is doing. . .a hint that a land life might be possible, though she has never said it outright in thirty years. At a small desk in the engine room, a chief engineer tunes out the roar of giant diesels and writes a letter to his daughter in Arkansas. How's the new grandson? Has she been by the old place to see her mother? In Crystal City a mother writes a letter to her son, a young deckhand. His father will have his time off the river for Christmas. It would be nice to have the whole family together this year. A river pilot thinks of his family and all the things he will say in his letter. But by the time his shift is over, he will be tired and asleep within minutes. The letter will wait another day.

And when the long wait is over, when a man gets to be home for a time, it is never the way he had thought it would be. Maybe the boy has the measles or he runs out to play with his friends before you've had a chance to see how much he has changed. There's shopping to be done, clothes to be washed, a birthday party coming on Saturday. And adjusting to sleeping in a stationary place takes time, days of getting used to the fact there is no place you have to go, no schedule to keep, no landing to make. Those first nights in a land-bed are too quiet for you to sleep, and when you do sleep you awaken suddenly at the time of the shift change from your last trip on the river!

"You get the worst of two worlds," says a young wife of a new river pilot. "You don't see each other for weeks at a time, then suddenly you are together twenty-four hours a day. Neither of those is good. The worst times are when you want to talk to your husband about a problem, ask his advice, and he is on the river. Sometimes there is nothing really important, but you just need a friend, someone to talk to. And just when you think you can't stand it any longer, you get a letter or a phone call and he says he's on his way home."

Eventually the land-life routine settles in, and you're glad to be home and an active part of the family again. But then comes the call; you have to catch the boat at St. Paul or Memphis or perhaps New Orleans.

"It's a life of good-byes for me," a towboat widow admits, "but my husband says its really a life of happy hellos."

Soon there would be the hellos for two river families. During the night, Kentucky had surrendered its banks to that of Tennessee; the wooded west bank of Missouri ended at Arkansas's northern river boundary; and by noon of our first day on the lower river, we had come within sight of Lower Chickasaw Bluff, the fourth and southernmost of a series of Tennessee cliffs. Here stands the city of Memphis, home of the blues and Beale Street (officially Beale Avenue). Here Jeff Mitchell and Keith Harris were to leave the *Harriet M* for their relief time.

When the two home-bound men boarded the store boat that had brought mail and provisions out to the *Harriet M*, every member of the crew, except for Buddy, who was piloting the boat, turned out on deck to see them off. The remaining crew traded whoops, hollers and catcalls with the men on the launch. The rowdy mood prevailed for a time, then wound down to an easy quietness as the small boat pulled further away from the *Harriet M* and moved closer to the bank.

Some of the men went directly to the kitchen to collect their mail, but a few stayed to look after the launch until it became lost in the busy river traffic of modern Memphis'

Wolf Harbor. Before he caught the bus for home, Jeff promised, he would mail the stack of letters Walter had given him. There was at least one message to home from every crewman, and two quickly penned notes from a hitchhiker with a slight case of the Fever.

The days aboard the *Harriet M* beat with a comforting repetition. At 5:30 a.m. the men working the six-to-twelve were awakened by a member of the night watch. After dressing quickly and coming sleepy-eyed to the kitchen, they would find Emma waiting to feed her hungry "family." There would be fresh pots of coffee already brewed (Emma always rose an hour before the men), hot and steamy homemade bread, breakfast sausages, ham and eggs any way a man desired, and fresh butter and jam to melt over a stack of fluffy hot cakes. The new shift ate quickly, usually managing to shovel down two helpings within twenty minutes. You have to be a riverman to do it. The weary graveyard shift, though, ate slowly and not as much, and rarely took coffee before they fell wearily into the sack. The scene was repeated at 11:30 a.m. and 5:30 p.m., at dinner and supper.

Each day was the same, and only by the meals did a man know what day of the week it was. Saturday, for example, was steak day. On Friday there was catfish. Golden brown chicken was on the table on Wednesday, and again on Sunday.

And between the meals there was the work. The river's locks were far behind us and there would be no more breaking the tow until we reached New Orleans. But each shift had its turn at "soochin'" the decks and windows. Hours had to be spent on the barges, checking and often tightening the thick wires that were in a constant tug-of-war with the river to keep the tow a possession of man. There was always line to be cut, spliced and rolled, and there was always scraping and painting to do.

And so each day passed as we moved steadily southward, now sailing the river's tortuous channel between the cottonwood lands of Mississippi and Arkansas. Here I felt I was in the real South, where the bright sultry days and the clear soft nights were sweet with the drug of flowering trees.

Between chores was for stern-line talk, story telling.

"That's somethin' that reminds me of the days I knew Johnny Cash, the singer," Arkansas Bill said as he came into the pilothouse one afternoon.

"Well, that somethin' musta been outside with you," Shelden teased; he knew Arkansas Bill was just looking to pass some timberhead talk. "You just got in here, ain't even got your tail in far enough to close the door, and I know there ain't nothin' in here to remind you of Johnny Cash."

In his slow, deliberate manner Arkansas Bill closed the door and slipped a small wrench into the back pocket of his overalls, which always sagged under the weight of one tool or another, even when he sat down to eat.

"That sick cow you're listenin' to croak on that radio what's reminded me," Arkansas Bill said. "Call that music?" He turned his towboat figure towards me and winked. "Don't pay that coonass pilot any mind, son. Coonasses are as dumb as they come and don't deserve no attention."

"I don't know about that," Shelden defended. "There ain't nobody in the world 'cept a coonass who can look at a whole field of rice and tell you just how much gravy you'll need."

Arkansas Bill laughed. "Anyways—"

Arkansas Bill: "Hurry it up, son—I got stories to tell."

"Now just how many days did you know Johnny Cash?" Shelden interrupted, figuring he would get the engineer started up about "coonasses," something Sheldon liked to do every chance he got.

But the engineer was wise to the pilot's tricks. "Just two that I want to tell about," he said, "and they was wide apart in years." Shelden kept quiet then, but the Memphis Sound coming from the radio filled the pilothouse.

"Anyways. . .that first day was back before I thought of ever coming to the river. My daddy took over the Cash place after they'd lost it; they were pretty poor in those days. Well, I was gettin' ready to chop some cotton when Johnny and a friend of his come along and says they want to work. 'Better work and not start foolin' in the field,' I told 'em. 'I ain't got but seventy-five cents in my pocket,' I says, 'so we better get enough cotton to the gin today if you want to get paid.' They was just boys then, didn't work much, and we never got to the gin in time." Arkansas Bill gave a chuckle. "Those boys. . .they didn't care 'bout that, and they chased me all over my daddy's fields until they got me down. They took the seventy-five cents and ran off. Never did come back to get the money I owed 'em."

Shelden guffawed. "I'll bet you weren't gonna pay 'em much more than that anyways."

"I sure woulda paid 'em good wages," Arkansas insisted. "But first I woulda give 'em a little lickin' for knockin' me down. And the next time I saw Johnny that's what almost happened," he told us. "He came to the house one day, wearing his Army uniform and just lookin' for trouble. Always wanted his daddy's place back, and he held it against us for havin' it. I says, 'If you want to fight, it's OK with me,' and I rolled up my sleeves," Arkansas Bill sat up straight and tucked in his stomach, as best he could. He had a towboat figure now, but I could see the hint of what was once a broad, thick Arkansas farm boy. "Well, he thought about it a minute," the engineer continued, "then picked up his bag and said, 'I don't want to get dirt on my uniform.' I never did see him again, but I'm glad he ain't poor no more, even if he never did get his daddy's place."

And late one night Herbie came into the pilothouse with a box. Inside were plates and two fresh pineapple pies, Buddy's favorite dessert.

"What's this for?" asked Buddy.

"Emma says this brings her up to date for last Thursday's game of rummy," Herbie said and passed out big slices of the cream-topped dessert to Buddy, Walter, Willie and me.

"That Emma is one hell of a cook," Buddy praised, opening the door to one of the favorite rooms of sternline talk for rivermen: river cooks.

"Sure is," Walter agreed. "But she'll be gettin' off soon, and who knows what we'll get then."

"I sure hope we don't get one like that old gal that made nothin' but beans. . . . I never knew there was so many kinds of beans till that gal laid 'em out there. Five bowls of beans at breakfast, then six or seven at dinner and supper. I was sure glad to see her go."

"At least beans are good for you," Walter said. "Got protein in 'em. Take them over strawberries any day."

"Godalmighty, Walter, don't even say the word strawberry." Willie slapped his knee and laughed. "Just hearin' that word makes me break out all over again. That gal put strawberries in everythin'. Got rid of that gal fast. In Memphis, wasn't it, Buddy?"

"St. Louis," Buddy said. "I was calling in an order when

she told me to get another case of strawberries. Fired her right there, helped her pack even. Ate cold sandwiches for ten days and loved every one of 'em.''

"That bald cook we had used to drive me nuts," Walter said. "I had to give her an extra closet just for all those wigs she had. I wouldn't have cared so much, but they was the real cheap kind and kept slippin' around on her head. Like to drive me crazy watchin' her cook and push her hair around. Fell over her eyes one time, and when she tried to move it, she got a fork stuck right in it and pulled it clean off."

Herbie handed out seconds and went on. "We had some real doozies all right. Remember that gal used to lick her lips all the time while she was cookin'? It used to bother me a little, so I stopped goin' to the kitchen when she was there. But then I stopped eatin' any cooked food when we found out she had gotten out of some nuthouse for tryin' to poison her husband."

Willie spoke up. "I'll never forget that one. She almost caused me to give up drinkin'. I'd just come on the boat, and I'd had a few before I reported. Well, she musta come on while I was sleepin'—"

Willie stopped talking then. Buddy had set aside his plate, sat up straight in the pilot's chair, and gripped the controls firmly. We were coming to the bridge just below Greenville, Mississippi, considered a danger to tows. It was this bridge that, on a cold night in March, 1948, had claimed the modern towboat *Natchez* and her 26-man crew. When divers were finally able to search for the boat and the thirteen men left on board, they were unable to find any trace of her.

We made an easy pass between the piers, and every man breathed easier. They all knew why they had kept silent during the passing. Buddy knew too, but no one even mentioned it. And Willie was eager to get on with his story.

"Well, sir, I went to the kitchen next mornin' and I was feelin' a bit cottonmouthed. I wasn't in condition for any shocks, that's for sure, but there she was. . .her chest big as milk jugs, wearin' one of them mini skirts and those red leather boots that went clear up to her kneecaps, and lickin' her lips at ninety miles an hour. I went to the hallway and thought about what I'd seen, then gave some thought, just a moment of thought mind you, to swearin' off the booze for good. But when I went back to the kitchen and saw her still standin' there big as life, I knew I'd need a drink the minute I got my next time off."

It was time for the shift to change, and Shelden came into the pilothouse to take the controls. "That Emma is a great cook," he said and patted his stomach, which was just beginning to tell of towboat cooking.

"She sure is," Herbie said. He got a second wind. "You wasn't on here then, but we had a cook one time. . . ." Buddy left the controls and went with me to the kitchen.

In the swifter current of the Lower Mississippi, we sped downriver at twelve miles an hour, past the boundary where Arkansas becomes Louisiana, beyond the mouth of the Yazoo River, and beneath the hills of Vicksburg, Mississippi. There, a little more than a hundred years ago, the gallant Confederate civilians and military men defended the key city to the Mississippi.

For forty-seven days the people and soldiers at Vicksburg suffered under Union cannons and a supply shortage. When all the food was gone, they slaughtered mules and nourished themselves on the sweet, tough flesh. Then only the city's rats remained. Traps were set and the small, fried bodies of the rodents were served to the beleaguered men, women, and children. Soon even this food was gone, and on July 4, 1863, General Grant accepted the unconditional surrender of Vicksburg.

The city had been defeated but the memory of that siege and the "damn Yankees" lingered on in deliberate protest for more than eighty years after the war. Until 1945, when Nazi Germany surrendered to the Allies, most of Vicksburg's citizens refused to celebrate Independence Day and treated July Fourth as any other day of the week. Today it is a very American city, though the relics of the siege—trenches and fortifications—are still enshrined in a Federal park behind the city.

And at Vicksburg is the bridge that crosses the Mississippi and links the city with the Louisiana Bank.

Shelden was on duty when we approached the most dangerous bridge for river pilots. He stood up from the pilot's chair, as he always did when he made a bridge or flanked a bend, and worked the levers hard, bringing the head of the tow to the right. To me it seemed that we were headed right for a pier and would ram the bridge.

"Looks bad, don't it?" Shelden said. I agreed. "But we're really in good shape," he assured me. "There's a strong set"—cross current—"here that comes off the right bank, and you have to aim right for that pier and let that set bring you over to port."

Following the instructions of his apprenticeship days, Sheldon continued to hold the tow at an angle to the pier. The current suddenly gripped our tow, as the pilot had promised, and moved us safely between the massive columns of steel and cement with just enough space so as not to scrape the paint.

And all this time I could see a salvage boat working to raise a broken barge whose nose pressed against a pier close to the right bank. I sighed in relief. So did Shelden.

Some seventy miles further downstream and three hours into night, we were sailing off the shore of Natchez. From the river, the city was only distant lights shining from the windows of a few indistinct buildings on top the 200-foot-high bluffs.

In the era of the great cotton planters, Natchez was small but elegant, with the stately columned mansions built and furnished in the best of European decor by their rich plantation owners. The number of millionaires in Natchez during its better days, by the way, was second only to that in New York. Those days of the "city on the hill" were ones of wide bustling streets with row after row of lush, shade-giving trees, well-established businesses, lawn parties on sultry afternoons, southern belles in hooped dresses, of chivalry and respectability.

The glory faded after the war, however, and only the recent discovery of rich oil and natural gas fields has brought back the golden age to Natchez. Her citizens have used the new-found wealth to restore and preserve many of the antebellum mansions: homes like Linden; Elmscourt; The Briars, where the beautiful Varina Howell lived and married Jefferson Davis; Longwood; Stanton Hill; Hope Farm, once the home of a Spanish governor; Elgin; Windy Hill Manor.

Though the river has claimed all but a few of the decaying brick buildings, the other Natchez—Natchez-Under-the-Hill—is still remembered. It lay under the bluff along the waterfront and was the Mississippi crossroads of the Natchez Trace, that ancient trail of Indians, traders, settlers and flatboatmen. The Trace ran from Natchez to Nashville and was a favorite raiding route for murderous thieves who waited to take the money and lives of Ohio Valley farmers who would raft their produce downstream, sell it and the rafts themselves, then travel home by foot or on horseback along the trail.

But sometimes Natchez-Under-the-Hill cheated the waiting highwaymen. With its staple of brothels, gambling halls, and saloons the town often claimed the virtue, money and life of many a farmer, traveler or riverman before he could begin the long journey home, and all in a reveling night's work. There were gouging matches and knife fights, many of which brutally ended with the knife of Jim Bowie.

Only the respectability at the top of the hill remains today, but the lusty hearts who preferred life under the hill and made possible the growth of commerce on the Mississippi in those days will not be forgotten.

On the run from Natchez to Baton Rouge, the river's vigorous current—twirling and drowning giant logs and stumps—twists through a monotonous landscape. For tens of miles at a stretch there is nothing but forest on either side of the stream. Then comes a bend and a clearing where cattle can be seen grazing on luscious grass. The river twists again and the forest returns, with not a house or a human in sight.

But on the river itself there is great activity, with the frequent passing of north- and southbound tows, their whistles blasting over their acres of barges. And by the time both east and west banks were Louisiana's, we began to pass the brown geysers spraying high above the river's surface from the long pipe-nostrils of dredges. And along the banks were armies of men and machines. Taking advantage of the summer's low water, they were laying giant steel and concrete mattresses that they hoped would hold the bank together when the next high water comes, as it surely will.

Where a man is not fighting the river, this vast flood plain is a refuge of solitude and peace, a treasure of wilderness beauty. Great clouds bend and fan the sun's rays into magnificent light storms over the river, and the air is soft and sweet.

By that afternoon, however, I began to notice a change in the air. We were slipping steadily into the haze and odor of modern industrial civilization. Baton Rouge.

When the early Frenchmen paddled upstream, what they saw first was a red stick, a *baton rouge*, a red-painted stick that marked a tribal boundary for the Indians. It was a good place for traders and settlers, rising high enough above the river to gain safety from all but the worst floods. Today it is still a good place, this time for an energy-seeking culture; for Baton Rouge lies in the middle of the rich oil fields of Louisiana, Mississippi, and Texas. From there pipelines nourish the petrochemical plants that turn out gasoline, jet fuel, and kerosene.

North of the city, huge circular oil storage tanks dominate the banks, and to either side of the river in the port itself, there are stacks and tubes and towers that totally dwarf the city's skyline. The murky water in the harbor is constantly boiling in the wake of tows and tugs, and anchored outside the channel that day or moored along the miles of wharves were the first big ships I'd seen on the river.

Some were anchored outside the channel, waiting to take their places at the loading docks where other ships flying the flags of many nations were being loaded with the goods of America, the bounty made possible by the river. Other ships—freighters and tankers—led the way south to New Orleans and the open sea.

Heading for New Orleans from Baton Rouge, the unbroken line of bankside levees face each other over a river that is now a half mile wide. Beyond the levees are large, flat patches of farmland, swamp and bayou. Looming over all of this for the 130 miles to New Orleans are the huge burn-off stacks, their flickering flames reddening on the surface of the rolling river.

The next morning, my twentieth day hitching the Mississippi, the *Harriet M* followed the channel to the port of New Orleans, the second largest port in the United States (New York-New Jersey being first). In living testimony to this fact, scores of tows and boats and ships move steadily north and south in the channel or rest along the banks, solid miles of docks and wharves, cranes and loading containers. Behind all of this rises the modern skyline of the new city: closer to the river are the elegant old buildings of the original Crescent City.

I stayed with the *Harriet M* for a few more hours while Buddy maneuvered in the busy harbor to unload our barges, then face up to a new tow to be moved over seventeen hundred miles upriver to St. Paul.

By that afternoon the new tow was ready; Walter, getting time off, was packing; new men, fresh from home, boarded to put in time on the river. It was time for me to leave the *Harriet M*. New Orleans is the southernmost great city on the Mississippi; but the river travels further south for more than another hundred miles, and I would have to find another ride if I was to make it to the sea, a place where towboats never tread.

The whole crew turned out on deck to see me off and wish me luck in hitching the homestretch to the sea. With a kiss from Emma, I climbed into a small outboard, and one of the new deckhands raced us downriver and toward the bank.

Half a mile down from where I left the *Harriet M*, the deckhand pulled to the bank, held her steady until I was safely ashore, then turned quickly and sped away. The feel of dry, steady land under my feet unnerved me. As I watched the boat heading upriver, I wished I could make the north-run with it. I would miss my river friends.

I couldn't have picked a better spot to land. Climbing the white rocks hugging the bank, I found myself at the foot of Jackson Square, the heart of the old city near the river. A block inland was the foot of St. Peters Street, crowded with dozens of artists displaying their creations to hundreds of tourists or painting portraits of these visitors to the "Paris of America."

Resting myself and my equipment (I'd forgotten its weight) at an outdoor cafe, I enjoyed the sharpness of dark chicory-enriched coffee and let the charm and magic of the French Quarter, or Vieux Carr (Old Square) come over me—the towers of St. Louis Cathedral looming over the square, the wrought-iron balconies, the facades of lace ironwork, the flower gardens, and the seductive beauty of the women who belonged to the Quarter.

I was filled with the *joie de vivre* that afternoon, but I had not yet earned my time off. There was still river to be seen, and I set about the near impossible task of getting a ride into the Gulf of Mexico.

As it is in Minneapolis, you can't stand on the bank of New Orleans and point your thumb southward. I remembered my lesson from those first days spent trying for a ride on the river, and I began making the rounds of the offices of towing and salvage companies, the Crescent City Pilot's Association, the Board of Commissioners of the Port of New Orleans (the

The Mayo Lykes, my last hitch downriver, begins her journey across the Atlantic.

Dock Board), and of the plush offices of a few steamship companies.

For nearly two days I tried in vain to secure my last ride, one that would bring me to the sea and, just as important, back again to the dry land of the continental United States. My request was met with surprise, perhaps a few odd glances, and admiration. Everyone I spoke to seemed genuinely interested in what I was trying to do, but there were problems: Private industry had problems with insurance companies who were never eager to have a passenger aboard a working vessel on the river, and, of course, there was the problem with unions if I wanted to work my way to the sea. The pilot's associations—there are several—needed permission from the ship's owners, something that would be impossible in the case of foreign vessels, which were in abundance in New Orleans. A steamship company needed permission from the pilot's association to let a passenger board a pilot boat.

It was a discouraging circle in which I spun until Kenneth Parker, an adventurous member of the Dock Board, decided he couldn't let me be stopped so close to my goal. He made the necessary phone calls and vouched for me. On the afternoon of my second day in New Orleans it was set; I had a ride to the sea on the *Mayo Lykes*.

With a complimentary ticket giving me passage from New Orleans to Pilottown, I boarded the 495-foot freighter owned by the Lykes Bros. Steamship Company, New Orleans, and was welcomed aboard and invited to a ship's dinner by Captain S. P. Anderson, a thirty year veteran of the sea. Bound for Casablanca and Algiers, Captain Anderson carried a cargo of over six thousand tons of flour and nearly two thousand tons of general cargo. And to the Gulf of Mexico he carried one hitchhiker.

In the early morning darkness of the following day, our upriver pilot climbed aboard and manned his duty station on the bridge. Commands went to the helmsman and to the deck. Mooring lines flew to the wharf, the ship's horns blasted, and the river bubbled and boiled at our stern as we slipped out into the deep channel to make our run to the sea.

As the 13-mile port area of New Orleans fell behind us, the lights of the city grew faint. They flickered like fireflies maddened with courtship and then finally faded in the climax of the blackness. Other great ladies of the sea, with the Mississippi cleansing their bows and carrying the salt back to the oceans, drifted mysteriously past us, their lights rolling over our port side. And on the bank of the coffee-colored river, caught briefly in the waving fans of light, live oaks and willows and cypresses stood like an army of lookouts for the levees guarding the precious land.

The land. In the beginning, a small string of river towns like Belle Chasse and Jesuit Bend, Bertrandville and Wills Point, Gloria and Carlisle stand on dry ground that stretches east and west for miles before surrendering to the inevitable marshes. But as the river pushes nearer and nearer to its submission to the sea, it seems to draw the land ever closer to itself, forcing the delta into marsh and a mosaic of out-of-river channels, lakes, bayous, swamps and sloughs.

As the *Mayo Lykes* put mile after mile behind us, we moved deeper into the paradoxical life of the river. Sixty miles below the Crescent City is Port Sulphur. Here a tiny range of sulphur-mountains shatter the natural flatness of the land. The air strikes the nostrils with an acid sting; and yet further downstream, on the same west bank, the village of Buras is surrounded with orange groves that in early spring perfume the air for miles around.

And the diversity of the river's banks is equally matched by the diversity of the people who live upon them. While farmers of French and German and Italian ancestry harvest Louisiana's golden fruit, which they will ship throughout the nation or press into a sweet heady wine, Manilamen, Chinese, Malays, Yugoslavs and a mixture of the races hunt, trap and fish in the wooded swamp and marshlands. Or from the banks and along the tidal bays of the bordering gulf, they will trawl for the gray shrimp and harvest the oyster beds.

If I wanted to tackle the question of Nature's indecision, I would do so here, in this strange and incredible region of the river: As the sun prepares to ride over the "land," a delta fisherman will hear a strange drumming sound. This sudden rumbling is startling to a stranger. It is the river's speech, according to the Indians, but the fisherman knows it is the sheep's head he may soon add to his catch. Then into his boat he may haul an eight-foot sturgeon or a sweet paddlefish. Or perhaps danger will come to the surface in the form of a winter visitor from the Sargasso Sea—an eel more than a yard long and equipped with jaws that will grip like steel. Or the water may explode around his boat with the thrashing of a shark-sized alligator gar, the most feared of Mississippi fish, a good one-quarter of its half-reptile body being ferocious jaws that have tasted all flesh—including man's.

All along this final stretch of the river, it was obvious that Nature was still deep in thought. By the time we reached Venice, Louisiana, the last solid ground on the Mississippi's southward course, the world had changed again. To port and starboard lay mist-covered, desolate green marshes that spoke forlornly of lonesomeness, and I felt as though our ship would be doomed in the last miles of the earth. But out there were the ideal habitats for hundreds of thousands of migratory waterfowl, and in the swamps behind the river live mink, otter, skunk, muskrat, and the coypu that gives delta trappers their prize nutria pelts.

All around there is beauty: lotus and water hyacinth, geese, ducks, and white herons; and there is fever, fury and sudden death: mosquitos, alligators and cottonmouths—gods, devils, and voodoo.

The *Mayo Lykes* slowed as we reached the small, stilt-supported settlement of Pilottown, where the two aristocracies of river pilots and bar pilots share the same catwalks. A small pilot boat came alongside and our upriver pilot, who would wait here for his turn to guide a northbound vessel to New Orleans, left our helmsman under the command of Captain John L. Levine, Sr. It was now the duty of this fifth generation bar pilot (his son was serving his apprenticeship) to guide us safely through the last twenty-two miles of the river's channel.

Underway again, Captain Levine navigated our freighter the few miles to the Head of Passes, where what little shore that was left suddenly shattered, spreading the river into wide gray arms. The channels are numerous—Dead Women Pass, Seven Pass, North Pass, Tiger Pass, Flatboat Pass—but only Pass a Loutre, South Pass, and Southwest Pass are considered to be main channels to the sea.

"We'll be taking Southwest Pass," Captain Levine told me. "It's the only one I trust now, and I think I'll be around till it gets too shallow for these big ships if the Engineers don't get onto it soon." He studied the river, then looked back to me. "South Pass was a good thirty feet not too long ago; now it's down to about eighteen or twenty feet. I don't like 'about' figures when I'm piloting a ship."

It was about a hundred years ago that James Eads, the same engineer who had constructed the first bridge to cross the Mississippi at St. Louis, undertook the monumental task of building the first in a series of jetties which the government hoped would force the river to cut and clean its own channel through South Pass. The river was at that time rapidly filling itself in with sand and mud, threatening to close its mouth to all seagoing traffic. It was a daring concept, but Eads went to work knowing that if he failed he would not be paid, an agreement he himself had offered to the government. The river did not submit easily, but in less than two years the pass began to deepen. The river had finally been forced to turn against itself. But the Mississippi is still a reluctant mistress to man's interest and commerce. The Corps of Engineers must continually keep the river from making islands of the modern-day jetties, then drowning them and thus filling up the channels.

Putting his "local knowledge" to work—"Left five!" he orders the helmsman, who repeats the command—our bar pilot moves us easily down the last twenty miles to the sea. The river's channel is still flanked by low-lying strips of marsh. And you can feel that the river does not want to die.

But soon there was a tang of salt, and the blue of the Gulf became visible. As we passed the aquatic Southwest Pass Bar Pilot Station and plowed beyond the river's mouth toward the sea buoy, the Mississippi's brown waters seemed to be trying to fight its way out across the sea to the other continents. For miles, the waters would still be brown and fresh. Creatures of the sea—porpoise, flying fish, gulls, pelicans—would swim and leap from the blue waters to the last brown surge of the dying giant.

Outside the hatchway to the bridge, Captain Anderson took an azimuth reading and prepared to take command of his ship. I looked out across our bow to the far horizon and drew in the salt air. My downriver journey had ended. In a little more than three weeks, I had come from the cool placid waters of Lake Itasca, mother of the Mississippi, to the rolling and choppy waters of the sea.

It is difficult to come to such a journey's end, and it was reluctantly that I followed Captain Levine down the ship's ladder and boarded the tiny pilot boat that would take us to the bar pilot station. Though there wasn't much time for celebration, Captain Anderson had the deep throats of the ship's horns blast a congratulation, a victory, as we slipped away and headed into the mouth of the river. From the wooden planks of the last outpost on the Mississippi, I waved my thanks and farewell.

It was time to go home. A crew boat from an oil rig came into the river later that day and a friendly riverman known only as "Cowboy" let me thumb a ride with him. There was still a lingering mist as we headed upriver toward dry land, but I could see beyond—all the way to the northern woods and the canoe trails. There were the locks and the dams, and the oxbows and the levees. On the river in my mind were the johnboats and the houseboats, the towboats and the tugs, the pirogues and the ships. I could see clearly the Chippewas and Scandinavians, the Irishmen and Germans, the French and Spanish. All are sharing their lifeblood with the lifeblood of the nation—the Mississippi, America's Father of Waters.

THE END

ACKNOWLEDGEMENTS

I wish to acknowledge my deepest appreciation to the people who have traveled with me through the odyssey of writing this book: to my close friend Joseph H. Polkowski, for his patient readings while this work was in progress; to Florence and Howard Linn Edsall, authors who so generously shared their time and knowledge; to Neil D. Schuster, of The American Waterways Operators, Inc., the staffs of the Newark Public Library and the Bloomfield Public Library, for their enthusiastic assistance with my research; to Al Giovinetto, of Lane Studios, for his photographic assistance; and to all the rivermen, especially those who have been so generous in giving me of their time and of their knowledge.

BIBLIOGRAPHY

Burman, Ben Lucien, *Big River to Cross: Mississippi Life Today*. New York: The John Day Company, 1938-39-40.

Carter, Hodding, *Man and the River: the Mississippi*. Chicago: Rand McNally & Company, 1970.

Clemens, Samuel Langhorne (Mark Twain), *Life on the Mississippi*. New York: Harper, 1917.

Clemens, Samuel Langhorne, *The Family Mark Twain*, which includes the complete Mark Twain books of *The Adventures of Tom Sawyer* and *The Adventures of Huckleberry Finn*. New York: Harpers, 1935.

Dobie, John, *The Itasca Story*. Minneapolis: Ross & Haines, Inc., 1959.

Hartsough, Mildred Lucille, *From Canoe to Steel Barge on the Upper Mississippi*. Minneapolis: University of Minnesota Press, 1934.

Havighurst, Walter, *Voices on the River*. New York: Macmillan, 1964.

Keating, Bern, *The Mighty Mississippi*. Washington, D.C.: The National Geographic Society, 1971.